CONVERSATIONS WORTH KEEPING

Getting to know the God who keeps
company with His creation

AMBER HOFLAND

ISBN: 1984316001
ISBN-13: 978-1984316004

CONTENTS

conversations worth keeping

This book, this collection of stories and reflections you're about to read, began as just that—reflections on God and the precious things in life. Each one came about through conversations with Jesus or conversations with others about Jesus, to which my heart or my friends said, "You need to write this down. You need to save this for later and forever. This is good for the rest of your life." I began taking notes on Jesus' work in my heart and ended up with a collection of conversations to remember.

I think conversation is where it all happens. I know that talk is cheap and conversation is nothing without action, but ours is a God who spoke creation. He spoke life into being when Father, Son, and Spirit made man in Their image. Scripture says Jesus is the Word of God. I love that. We always think of the Bible when we talk about reading the Word of God, but John calls Jesus the Word, as if Jesus is what God said to us. And if Jesus is the Word, and we are made in His likeness, we are like little words. We are conversations. We are the only things in all of Jesus' creation capable of speaking language. Oceans, stars, trees, animals—they don't speak language to each other or to God, but we were made in the likeness of the Word. We were made in conversations, as if our very likeness screams out that God wanted to converse with, interact back and forth with us.

The popular evangelical Christian phrase is that God wants relationship, not religion. And what is relationship without conversation? Every relationship of any kind starts with and is continued by a conversation. No husband and wife go from being strangers who meet once and talk for an hour in a coffee shop to becoming spouses unless, at some point along the line, the conversation continues. And spouses don't get through life and its hurdles—awkwardness, tension, frustration, misjudgments, misunderstanding, hurt feelings, conflict, brokenness, betrayal—unless the conversation continues. Relationships don't exist after those things unless someone says, "We're going to keep talking through the uncomfortable," and the other agrees. But as long as that conversation continues, as long as we keep talking, we can get through those things; whatever they are, we can work them out.

I think all Jesus wants from us, His conversations, is to keep talking with Him through the clashes and the chaos, the things that don't make sense to us and the things we think we know already. He wants to keep having this conversation with us for all of eternity, because if we do that, if we keep talking with Him, He can work out everything else in us. He can let His good news permeate our hearts and work all the way through as long as we continue our conversation with Him.

Oh, how the Word longs to keep conversation with His likeness-made. Yes, He made you and me little words in His likeness, because we are His "Write this down." His "Save this for later and forever." His "This is good for the rest of your life." Dear reader, you and me—we are His conversations worth keeping.

> *Then God said, "Let us make man in our*
> *image, after our likeness..." So God created*
> *man in his own image, in the image of God*
> *he created him; male and female*
> *he created them.*
> *Genesis 1:26-27*

> *In the beginning was the Word, and the*
> *Word was with God, and the Word was*
> *God. He was in the beginning with God.*
> *All things were made through him, and*
> *without him was not any thing made*
> *that was made.*
> *John 1:1-3*

His best shot

I had no idea what I was doing, honestly. A two-subject pencil portrait was far more demanding than my little penguin and record player sketches, but I wanted to make something for a beautiful friend, hoping that it would blow her and her groom away. Here's the thing—even in its frame, there are a thousand things I would change. It's so close to looking like the original photo of the bride and groom, but it's not exact. But as a creative, I have had one rule for anything I make or do, which is always to let it be beautiful; albeit imperfect, just let it be beautiful.

As I was reflecting on why I love the drawing so much, despite the inevitable insecurities that accompany the courage I could muster to share it with my dear friend as a wedding gift, I think it comes down to this: I gave it my best shot.

People talk about how the Lord loves us even though we're imperfect and we don't deserve it because that's just who He is—He is love. I once heard someone call it a "just because" love.

I think it's a "because" love, though. And I think the "because" is that He gave us His best shot. He spent immeasurable amounts of time dreaming us up and working us into existence. He didn't just find us and decide to keep us—He hand-wove His heart into ours. And beyond making us in His likeness with only qualities beautiful enough to be duplicated in creation, He dreamed—I mean, sat and stirred and racked His brain in the most exhilarating way—what He wanted to make us look like.

"This one will be quiet but vibrant with all the colors. This one will be bold but with meekness for her own good. This one will be a giver of laughter like honey and grace like water. This one will put you in your place with words that pierce but heal."

He spent eternity thinking of how lovely He wanted to create us, with exactly which materials and colors and dimensions. And when creation fell and imperfection hit, He was far too invested in His heart-stirred and brain-racked dreams to leave them unfinished or alone. He keeps giving them His best shot.

In the middle of our imperfections, He picks us up, and continues to create and recreate His dreams until they look more and more like the original. Just as I tweaked my portrait so that her nose would be lower and his eyes would be smaller to match the picture I was referencing, the Lord refines us overtime, saying, "Her heart should be bolder; his heart should be gentler; they should know grace and patience and trust..." until we start to look and feel like His absolute best shot. And that, I imagine, is a never-ending pursuit, presumably belonging to eternity.

But in the process—in between being a good shot and His best shot—He knows the beauty of what He is making. Every stroke is enchanting and noteworthy, because even in the beginning lays the *anticipation* of His best shot. He just knows it is going to be good, and He can't help but love it from the moment pencil meets paper.

And even though I put mine in a frame because my best shot reached its limits, His never does. He keeps creating gold in our hearts until only He knows when.

But even as we stand in our not-quite-right forms, we remain the all-of-His-might creations of an Almighty God.

For you formed my inward parts;
you knitted me together in my mother's
womb. I praise you, for I am fearfully and
wonderfully made. Wonderful are your
works; my soul knows it very well. My
frame was not hidden from you, when I
was being made in secret, intricately
woven in the depths of the earth.
Psalm 139:13-15

And we all, with unveiled
face, beholding the glory of the Lord,
are being transformed into the same
image from one degree of glory to
another. For this comes from the
Lord who is the Spirit.
2 Corinthians 3:18

create, swoon, rest

I think I started to understand Jesus better when I made my first quilt. I have always been a creative and a maker of various kinds of art, but there is something different about those things you can't make in a day—the ones that literally *must* take a long time to create. Those take-off-your-shoes, roll-up-your-sleeves, this-is-going-to-take-awhile kind of things are something special.

The night I finished piecing together the handkerchiefs in my first quilt, I spent fifteen minutes just sitting on the floor at 1 a.m. staring at it. I was beyond exhausted, but I couldn't believe how beautiful it was, and I couldn't believe I had made it—I had never made anything like it. So I sat there and swooned a little bit, letting it sink in. Then I went to sleep—something that is hard for me to do when my mind is still creating after my hands take a break.

Creating, as invigorating as it is, takes a lot out of you. Most good things do. And God doesn't grow tired, but still He rests. He lingers; He takes it in; and He swoons. He sits on the floor at 1 a.m. looking over His creation, saying,

"My, my, this is good." Then He rests. And the next day, I imagine He pours a cup of coffee just because He likes it, and He rolls up His sleeves and gets back to work—His good, beautiful, swoon-worthy work. Maybe it's not making a quilt or any other tangible piece of art; maybe it's making relationships and commitments, making goals, and making good on promises, but whatever we're making, let us not forget to take it in, to take a minute, and to swoon a little bit. And when we're finished, let's rest. Then, let's keep creating and swooning and resting, in that sweet, sweet order.

*And God saw everything that he had made,
and behold, it was very good. And there
was evening and there was morning, the
sixth day. Thus the heavens and the earth
were finished, and all the host of them.
And on the seventh day God finished his
work that he had done, and he rested on
the seventh day from all his work
that he had done.
Genesis 1:31-2:2*

unapologetically

I create things vigorously. My best friend tried to explain to someone my tendency to work on a project for hours at a time without breaks—something that doesn't feel burdensome to me in the slightest. She said, "It's intense." And I found myself saying, "I know; I have a problem." But as the words left my mouth, something in my heart hurt a little bit. The truth is, I love creating things. I love losing track of time and watching a project progress without delay. It's not always that I'm impatient; it's just that I love what I do. I love making things from scratch and watching raw materials come to life in a new form, and to hear myself refer to it as a "problem" felt wrong from the moment I said it.

Jesus made me creative—intensely creative. I think He loves that about me, and I think He gets it because He is Creator, too. I don't think He ever apologizes for that trait or that gift or for me. And because Creator made me unapologetically, I have no business apologizing for someone else's handiwork.

When I make something, I know the things about it that no one else knows. I know what it looked like in every stage of the process. I know how I got it to what it is now. I know where I hid the seams in the fabric lining and the four different versions of the same line I had in a song before it became the rhyme it is now. I know what I create intimately, and so does Jesus. And He never apologizes for or belittles His work. He doesn't introduce us as, "These are My creations, but they're small and flawed and they misunderstand a lot of things." No, He calls us, "My workmanship, My masterpieces, My 'very good.'" And if Creator doesn't apologize for His good work in us, by the grace of God, may we not either. When apology is due for the things of our own doing, we may by all means claim our imperfections, but apologize for the work of His doing? Never.

For you formed my inward parts;
you knitted me together in my mother's
womb. I praise you, for I am fearfully
and wonderfully made...
Psalm 139:13-14

For we are his workmanship, created in
Christ Jesus for good works, which God
prepared beforehand, that we
should walk in them.
Ephesians 2:10

the kitchen floor version

It may be the singer/songwriter in me, but nine times out of ten, I prefer music acoustic and unplugged. I prefer what I call a kitchen floor version of a song—the way the song feels when it is first written on the kitchen floor of a quiet house. Nothing beats that, to me. Nothing beats the first cut, the raw and intimate original with all of its heart and intent when thoughts first take their places in verses and lyrics first meet melody. A single instrument and a single voice playing music fresh off the presses of the heart—nothing beats that power.

When I recorded the songs on my EP, that is the version I wanted to capture. But here's the other thing about the kitchen floor version—you can hear everything. You can hear all of the intricacies in the music, including the ones that are less than perfect—the finger slips that make the high E string ring ever so slightly on the last C chord; the floor pedal beating to tempo during the rests where the piano is still fading out; and the simplicity of the instruments that make the vocals sound closer—like they're inches away from your ear. That's the kitchen floor version when recorded—unmasked, meek, and close enough to hear the details. And that kind of music, original and untouched, is trustworthy.

I think Jesus is the kitchen floor version—full of all power and all heart. No filters, no pretenses, no show. He gives it all and bears it all. And His heart is still enough to hear a pin drop. It doesn't miss a thing. It delights in the small and simple but extraordinary, the raw and intimate and inches from your ear. It is original and untouched and trustworthy.

> *Am I a God at hand, declares the LORD,*
> *and not a God far away? Can a man hide*
> *himself in secret places so that I cannot*
> *see him? declares the LORD.*
> *Jeremiah 23:23-24*

> *The LORD is near to all who call on him, to*
> *all who call on him in truth.*
> *Psalm 145:18*

> *Take my yoke upon you, and learn from*
> *me, for I am gentle and lowly in heart,*
> *and you will find rest for your souls.*
> *Matthew 11:29*

the dressmaker & the dress wearer

I put it back on the rack and walked about five feet before turning around to pick it up and admire it again. I was inexplicably drawn to this odd little 1960s style vintage silk dress and coat set in a color somewhere between yellow and green with beading that probably used to look silver but had turned black. There was something so strange and special about it that I didn't want anyone else to buy it. I didn't know where I'd ever wear it, but I wanted to take it home with me.

As I was taking out beads and seams to adjust it, I realized that the dress was custom-made. The tag, which was hand-stitched to the dress and contained no size information, said, "originals," an Italian surname, and "New York – Detroit." I wondered about the person who made the dress and how long it took to hand-stitch the beading. I wondered if the dressmaker designed it out of his or her own imagination or if the client gave exact instructions of what she wanted. I wondered about the woman for whom it was made. I wondered if she was an elitist socialite type, or if she was humble. I wondered what her reaction was when she first saw it and if she appreciated the dressmaker's work the way she should have.

I have made enough things in this life to know that the dressmaker always intends more than the dress wearer, the artist more than the person with a canvas on the wall, and the songwriter more than the listener could ever understand. That is the kind of Jesus we have—One who intends far more than we could ever fathom. In every single thing He touches and creates and multiplies into a thousand somethings, there is more of His breath than we dare to know. And while we put on a dress, hang a canvas, or listen to a song for the first time, seemingly out of nowhere, He steps back and watches us discover the idea He always had. Oh, how I want to just take a minute to turn around and admire His handiwork before picking it up and taking it home with me.

> *For the LORD is a great God, and a*
> *great King above all gods. In his hand are*
> *the depths of the earth; the heights of the*
> *mountains are his also. The sea is his, for*
> *he made it, and his hands formed*
> *the dry land.*
> *Psalm 95:3-5*

> *When I look at your heavens, the work of*
> *your fingers, the moon and the stars, which*
> *you have set in place, what is man that you*
> *are mindful of him, and the son of man*
> *that you care for him?*
> *Psalm 8:3-4*

sourdough starters & savoring

There are few foods I love more than sourdough bread. I was craving it on one of those "not leaving the house for anything" days, and I wanted to make some at home on a whim. Turns out, you don't make sourdough bread on a whim. I found out that it takes days or weeks to make the starter (the yeast mixture that makes the bread sour). The only way to expedite the process is to already have a starter ready.

Sometimes walking with Jesus feels like craving sourdough, and He's all like, "Hold on, first we have to make a starter." Or like when we're listening to a vinyl record, and we're three songs away from the one I want to hear, but dad always says albums were meant to be played all the way through. But despite my naturally impatient tendencies, I have become convinced that all the best meals take the longest to make and that albums are, in fact, better that way.

Though most of the time I am a spontaneous eater, not a preplanned meal maker, and my flesh itches for instant gratification and expedited processes, cooking with

Jesus is always about savoring, not shortcuts. There are no microwaves in Jesus' kitchen, but there's Jesus, and man, does He make good stuff. And sometimes He goes, "Come here; I'll chop, you stir." And sometimes He goes, "Put the spoon down; let's dance." But either way, He's not in a hurry. He savors every step of the process we spend with Him.

I want to savor with Jesus—not just the meal, but the making of it, too. I want to savor every moment and never be restless, because creating something good with Jesus is better than anything else; it just is.

"I am the living bread that came down from heaven. If anyone eats of this bread, he will live forever. And the bread that I will give for the life of the world is my flesh."
John 6:51

better than a roadmap

Sometimes we feel like Jesus is a secret-keeper. Like when parents are whispering to each other, and you ask what they are talking about, and they say, "Oh, it's nothing," when it is clearly not nothing, or "We'll tell you later," which is sometimes just a way of saying, "It's truly none of your business." I hate that. And sometimes, walking with Jesus feels like that—like He's whispering things and working on things and just leaving me out of it.

But there are a few things I know about Jesus. I know that His secrets are good ones, even though they can feel like avalanches He saw coming and didn't warn us about. I know that He knows what He's doing, even when we don't. And I know that it is not in His nature to exclude.

Sometimes we think Jesus is holding out on us— that He's not telling us things and it must be for our good. But really, I think He loves us too much not to tell us the truth, and we just take longer to process it. He's working diligently because He loves us too much to just give us what we think we want. And it's not because He's slow. It's because we are. We're trying to hurry Him along, but really,

I think we're the ones stalling the progress because we keep interrupting Him with our predictions.

My mom has this way of trying to finish my sentences when I'm in the middle of a story and always guessing wrong. We can be like that with Jesus. He starts from the beginning so we'll understand the full picture, and we want to know how it ends after the first three sentences. And He's like, "Wait, don't miss this. You need this middle part or it won't make sense." But He doesn't keep things from us. I think He's trying to tell us everything and not leave anything out. But we like endings, and He likes middles. He likes the thick of it and the still developing stories that are too rich for taking in all at once, that have to be savored. He likes the smack dab middle because that's where He gets to hang out with us. That's where He is God with us—not God ahead of us who leaves us behind and fills us in later, but God with us. And though we may not know the end of the sentence until we hear it, we are always going to know Him, the God who is with us in the middle of every story, and He is better than a roadmap, by far.

*No longer do I call you servants, for the
servant does not know what his master is
doing; but I have called you friends, for all
that I have heard from my Father I have
made known to you.*
John 15:15

*Think over what I say, for the Lord will
give you understanding in everything.*
2 Timothy 2:7

I will ask the Father, and he will give you
another Helper, to be with you forever...
You know him, for he dwells with you
and will be in you. I will not leave you as
orphans; I will come to you. Yet a little
while and the world will see me no more,
but you will see me. Because I live, you also
will live. In that day you will know that I
am in my Father, and you in me, and I in
you... the Helper, the Holy Spirit, whom the
Father will send in my name, he will teach
you all things and bring to your
remembrance all that I
have said to you.
John 14:16-20, v. 26

jam sessions & the Music-Maker

There is something about jam sessions that seizes my heart and makes it giddy. As a musician, I wish I'd have more of them, but as a singer-songwriter, I do most of my music-making alone. But there's something about jamming with another person that is unrehearsed, unmapped, ordinary, mistake-filled magic. One person starts playing something, and the other person joins in. That is one of my favorite things in the world—joining in. How beautiful it is to let people just sing or play in their own beauty, to just be as radiant as they are, and to join them after a little bit, when you find a way how. Be it with a harmony as voices and notes move together in sync, or with fingerpicking riffs that carry a melody of their own—what a delight it is to just join in on the song, on the beauty, on the goodness.

It baffles me to no end that the God of the universe sings songs over us, rejoices over us, delights in us. And if there is anything I know about God, it's that He makes good, good music. And we, with our unorganized, clumsy techniques, get to join in on the jam session with the Music-Maker. We get to show up, find a place, and jump in on the song. And in this life, we get to experience the impromptu, messy, and disordered wonder of making sweet, sweet sounds with a God who rejoices over us.

The LORD your God is in your midst, a
mighty one who will save; He will rejoice
over you with gladness; He will quiet you
by His love; He will exult over you
with loud singing.
Zephaniah 3:17

Jesus' yes

When I was teaching English at a summer camp in South Korea to a class of elementary and middle school aged children, in the middle of juggling lesson plans and skit rehearsals, I was reminded of the many reasons I think Jesus loves children so much. From their tireless appetite for all of the hand clap games I could remember from my own childhood to their headstrong desires to teach me their favorite dance moves and their persistent pleading to see me do a cartwheel in class, I found myself unable to say no to these kids.

One day with the elementary class, I came back from a snack break and found my students standing in the hallway to greet me, or rather, to push me away from the door. "Teacher, teacher, wait, wait!" they shouted, laughing. When I finally pushed my way through the giggling children and got inside the classroom, I could see that more of them were hiding something in the corner of the room. I looked suspiciously at them, thinking, "Oh no, what am I going to find over there, where the unsupervised children are snickering?" But after not being able to hold their giggles in any longer, they emptied grocery bags with chips and drinks for the whole class, held them up, and said, "Surprise party!"

My boys went to the little snack shop on campus, bought snacks for everybody, and organized a party, which incidentally was a surprise to only me. While I stood there, jaw-dropped in disbelief, they pushed their desks together to make a big table, and all of a sudden, we were laughing and snacking and surprise-partying. I was so blown away by their beautiful hearts that there was no part of me that wanted to make them do anything but have a surprise party. Even though we were supposed to run our skit lines for the performance two days later, the best thing to do in that moment was most definitely to have a party, and they knew that.

I know Jesus tells us to be the children, but sometimes I think Jesus has a child's heart. Sometimes there are surprise parties and impromptu fellowshipping or breaking the rules that Jesus wants to say yes to, and when He does, there's just nothing about Jesus' yes that I want to say no to. And much like my South Korean surprise-party-throwing students, Jesus' yes is always the best thing we could possibly do. If we knew the goodness Jesus has behind the door, the rich community that He's hiding in the corner, the not-in-our-lesson-plan conversations we're about to have, we couldn't help but say yes to them.

Granted, sometimes His surprises don't feel like snacks and a party—sometimes they feel like the last place we wanted to be—but even so, I have found that Jesus only has better for us. He only dreams what is better than our dreams, and He only gives what is better than we think we want. I'm convinced that if we knew the gold He has in mind for us, we'd never settle for silver again. And if we knew the things Jesus wants to say yes to, we couldn't help but say yes to them, too.

> *For my thoughts are not your thoughts,*
> *neither are your ways my ways, declares*
> *the Lord. For as the heavens are higher*
> *than the earth, so are my ways higher than*
> *your ways and my thoughts than your*
> *thoughts.*
> *Isaiah 55:8-9*

an empty bed instead

Before my semester in South Africa, in which I wouldn't know a single person in my cohort, I had been praying for my future roommate for months. Who you are with tends to shape your experience either positively or negatively, and I was going to have the absolute perfect and very well prayed for roommate. Nevertheless, I was the last person's name read on the rooming list, and I was given a room by myself. John Wilson 4. Two beds and all, just for me. It was ironic, confusing, and disappointing.

Before long, however, I found out why I was given John Wilson 4 instead of a roommate—I got to share it. John Wilson 4 became home to so many friendships, life-giving conversations, silly moments, worship sessions, homework parties, therapeutic rants, and movie nights. That extra bed was everybody's—from sleepovers to mega-beds to study couches, we called it "the guest bed," and that room was a sanctuary. I'd come back from class to find people there, working or sleeping or skyping. There was an open invitation with or without my presence. One friend called it a blessed room; another said she thought better in there. I didn't have a roommate, but that bed was rarely empty, and I always had someone to say goodnight to after pillow talk.

One day, I looked up from my laptop and counted eight other people working on papers in that little room. It was a miracle that we all fit. I remember laughing in that moment and saying to the Lord, "And I was worried about not having a roommate." That's the thing about God—He sees our prayers and their answers differently than we do. He did give me that roommate I prayed for so often, in the form of more than I could have even thought to pray for. Like an "I'll do you one more," He gave me an empty bed instead, and I pictured Him chuckling, or giving a wink, and saying, "I thought you'd like it better this way."

As you do not know the way the spirit
comes to the bones in the womb of a child,
so you do not know the work of God who
makes everything.
Ecclesiastes 11:5

painting with elephants

There is a painting in my room that my mom's friend brought back from Thailand when I was waiting to hear if I'd be receiving a grant to teach English there for a year. It was painted by an elephant, which meant even more to me than the fact that it was from Thailand. I told Jesus when we were on safari in South Africa that I want to ride elephants in Heaven. I thought, "Lord, if I could picture paradise with You, we'd be traversing Your creation sitting atop these grand and beautiful creatures. They'd be our mode of transportation." In Thailand, people do ride elephants, and I was certain that once I moved there, I'd get to do the same.

I didn't get the grant or go to Thailand, but I love seeing that painting every day because it reminds me of everything that has happened instead, which has been way too precious to miss. It reminds me that Jesus is here, exactly here, and not a millimeter off, and that wherever in the world I am, Jesus is the adventure. It reminds me that He knows my heart by heart and He specializes in making it dance. And it reminds me that I don't have to be afraid of being wrong about things like my future plans because the grace of God will make a fool out of me anyway.

Jesus has a way of taking our ideas, our dreams, our plans, and turning them into art of an *entirely* different genre. He takes our quests for whirlwind and paints whimsy instead. He sees our biggest dreams and illustrates the grandness of the small things, while also reminding us of the wonder of Him if ever our sense of adventure shrinks. He took my dream of riding an elephant in Thailand and gave me a picture painted by one to hang on my wall in the last place I ever thought I'd be instead. But rather than cringing from the awkwardness of almost moving to Thailand and riding an elephant, I smile when I see that painting on my wall, because it is a portrait of the adventure of Jesus, whose dreams blow mine out of the water every time. When I like black and white and things that make sense, He paints with colors—all of them, and He paints with elephants, too.

"Be still, and know that I am God.
I will be exalted among the nations,
I will be exalted in the earth!"
Psalm 46:10

let them be wildflowers

I love flowers, and I love surprises. I don't think they should be reserved for special occasions. I think we should have flowers and surprises on Thursdays, on our worst days, and on the regular ones, too. Handpicked bouquets on pillows, single stems on office desks, miniature arrangements in mason jars on doorsteps—there's nothing like it.

I live in a suburban beach city, and I couldn't tell you where wildflowers are around here. I Googled it one time in a desperate attempt to find and pick some, which is laughable now. But any flowers you see for picking belong to private property or city property in these parts, which means they're off limits.

It's strange to me—when this whole thing started and Jesus breathed life into the world, all flowers were wildflowers. They didn't belong to anyone, and no one paid for them. I'm pretty sure the rain watered them, not flower growers who make a living off of what has become a science. They were just there for everybody, like the Northern Lights before glass igloo hotels. I know we've come a long way since the days of "Let there be light and flowers," but how I wish we'd never forget that this good, good, beautiful creation was meant to be wild—to infiltrate every inch and every heart. It was designed that we may pick from it, grab ahold of it, wear it on our heads, and spread it around. From flowers to the Northern Lights, this good, good creation and the God who breathed it were meant to be for everyone to touch and feel and interact with. Perhaps the next time we hold our flowers, we'll remember they were wild once, and they came from a God who still is—One who is ours for the picking and grabbing ahold of.

The God who made the world and everything in it, being Lord of heaven and earth, does not live in temples made by man, nor is he served by human hands, as though he needed anything, since he himself gives to all mankind life and breath and everything. And he made from one man every nation of mankind to live on all the face of the earth, having determined allotted periods and the boundaries of their dwelling place, that they should seek God, and perhaps feel their way toward him and find him. Yet he is actually not far from each one of us...
Acts 17:24-27

i'm a parrot, and you're a falcon, 'kay?

I was walking home from the library on my college campus one night, and these two little girls whom I'd guess were about seven or eight years old were running around in long pretty dresses, sweaters, and sparkly shoes. One of them said to the other one, "I'm a parrot, and you're a falcon, 'kay?" The other one said, "Okay!" and they proceeded to run around flapping their arms in their long pretty dresses with their families twenty feet behind them. As I watched, the biggest smile crept onto my face because I remember what it was like to have an unconstrained imagination and how easy it used to be to just go with it.

When God says to come to Him like a child, I think this is part of it. I think it's like running around with your best friend in pretty dresses and sparkly shoes, flapping your arms because she said you're a falcon and you wouldn't want to be anything else. You don't even care that parrots are more colorful than falcons, because if she said she's a parrot and you're a falcon, so be it.

I think God starts running, and He looks back at us and says, "I'm your father, and you're My child, 'kay?" And,

"We're going to start flapping our arms like this now, 'kay? But no matter what, it's going to be great because we're best friends." And we watch our Best Friend start flapping and running, and all we want to do is the same exact thing, as peace and excitement simultaneously come out as "okay."

> *Jesus said, "Let the little children come to me and do not hinder them, for to such belongs the kingdom of heaven."*
> *Matthew 19:14*

babies getting glasses

There is a YouTube video of a little baby getting glasses and seeing her parents for the first time. There are so many things that just get me in this video—like the medical technology and know-how to prescribe eye glasses to an infant and the instantaneous effect as her whole face lights up with something indescribable at the clear image of her mom for the first time. She knows her mom very well— she knows her voice and her smell and her footsteps when she walks in the room in the mornings. And dad, too—she knows his kisses and his laugh and his belly-raspberries. But she hadn't seen the curve of their smiles or the love pouring out from their eyes. And when she did for the first time, it was overwhelming and uncontainable. The kind of uncontainable my cousins saw in their dog when he got lost at a neighbor's farm six miles away and they showed up to get him. He recognized them before they even got out of the truck and just kind of lost it with excitement.

I imagine that's what it's like to see God's face for the first time. I imagine we're just going to lose it—like a baby with glasses seeing the parents she knows with clear eyes for the first time, or a dog recognizing his owners from yards away after being lost on a different farm. But in something of a miracle, we also get to recognize God now. We get to know Him so intimately that our hearts recognize His—so we just know it when we see it. And even if we've never seen Him do something before, we know it's exactly something He would do—it's just got Him written all over it. We get to know Jesus like that.

For now we see in a mirror dimly, but then
face to face. Now I know in part; then I
shall know fully, even as I have been
fully known.
1 Corinthians 13:12

And we know that the Son of God has come
and has given us understanding, so that we
may know him who is true; and we are in
him who is true, in his Son Jesus Christ. He
is the true God and eternal life.
1 John 5:20

bugles & crayons

I made my best friend come over because I didn't know how to handle the epiphany exploding in my head. We sat on the floor eating Bugles and drew diagrams, word pictures, and definitions in crayon for hours as we unpacked the realization that everything I ever thought about love had to be wrong if God is love. For awhile, I considered it the day I met Jesus because prior to that day and that conversation, I didn't understand a thing about the Lord's patience, kindness, generosity, and refusal to take or hold captive.

Since that day, my best friend and I have had a few of what we call "Bugles and Crayons" moments, in which we discover something new about a God we've known for years, and we sit, mind-blown and head-reeling at the wonder of a God who loves us despite how little we understand about Him. And no matter how many epiphanies or discoveries about His character, we never run out of more Jesus to sink into. We never run out of things we thought we knew feeling truly concrete for the first time, and no matter how many times this happens, it feels like meeting Jesus again.

I think Jesus lives for those Bugles and Crayons moments. I think they light up His eyes like fireworks and strike strings like symphonies in His heart. I think He busts out dancing to the sound of His little ones finding Him overwhelmingly, unthinkably ravishing. Because that's the Jesus I know—One who sits on the floor with Bugles and Crayons with His children, reveling at the wonder of things deeper than a heart could ever know. Yes, I think He Bugles-and-Crayons like the best of them.

Can you find out the deep things of God?
Can you find out the limit of the Almighty?
It is higher than heaven—what can you do?
Deeper than Sheol—what can you know?
Its measure is longer than the earth
and broader than the sea.
Job 11:7-9

Jesus at a 5K

My sweet friend and I sat outside eating pizza and drinking carbonated juice the night before the 5K we made each other sign up for. We are what you would call un-athletic. As we talked about how unprepared we were to run the 5K, which we said we would not walk, and how little we had trained—trust me, if we had run it, we would have needed to train—one of us had the brilliant realization that Jesus knows we're not runners. We tried to imagine what Jesus would do at a 5K, and we made a new agreement.

We both thought of Jesus as a lingerer—a person who takes His time. So we decided we could linger, too. And we both thought He would be encouraging. So we vowed to encourage as many people as we could. As it turned out, we ended up mostly encouraging the people who had put on the event, rather than the runners who were all ahead of us, but it was by far the most fun I've ever had at a 5K.

The realization later dawned on me that Jesus likes to do everything with the ones He loves. He likes to run 5Ks with some people. He likes to sing and journal with people like me and play soccer with people like my best friend. He likes to fix things and run electrical wire with my brother, and He likes to listen to music with my dad. He runs and swims and cycles with triathletes and Olympians. And at a 5K, He is first place and last place and woke-up-at-5-am-to-be-here. Whatever our favorite thing to do is, my guess is that it's Jesus' favorite thing to do with us, too. Because that's the kind of Jesus He is—One who is with us, doing it, too.

"Behold, the virgin shall conceive and bear
a son, and they shall call his name
Immanuel" (which means,
God with us).
Matthew 1:23

And behold, I am with you always,
to the end of the age.
Matthew 28:20

giraffes & elephants & zebras, oh my

While my teammates painted flowers and grass and a tree that reached the ceiling, I painted the giraffe, elephant, and zebra. The giraffe was my height, and the zebra came up to my knee, but to a toddler, my cartoon animals may as well have been the life-sized ones I saw a few weeks earlier out in the South African bush. The day the little ones got to see the newly painted preschool playroom for the first time, they were so excited that they ran back and forth across the wall, trying to pet and kiss the animals. It was an overwhelming kind of moment for everyone in the room. Jumping, screaming, laughing, and big, round eyes filled with wonder created a chaos that somehow felt gleefully and familiarly like the comfort of home.

Children have this unmatched capacity for uncontainable excitement that I know gets Jesus in His core. I imagined the Lord watching His little ones lay eyes upon life like a mural He painted while we were sleeping. I imagined us running up to it and touching it to try to grab ahold of it ourselves. I imagined us standing two-feet tall at the bottom of a wall-sized wonder, blown away by how small we are next to it, but thrilled beyond measure to grow into it someday.

I felt this when we went on safari in the South African bush and saw nature untouched, the way I imagined it looked the very first week of creation. And I felt it when we painted preschool walls. Jesus dreams in colors and animals, flowers and clouds. He dreamt them up once, and He dreams them up still—sweet, sweet, wondrous things for us, who, like children, nap and toddle and who, hopefully, do not try to contain the excitement of laying eyes on the things He has done.

> *At that time the disciples came to Jesus,*
> *saying, "Who is the greatest in the kingdom*
> *of heaven?" And calling to him a child, he*
> *put him in the midst of them and said,*
> *"Truly, I say to you, unless you turn and*
> *become like children, you will never enter*
> *the kingdom of heaven. Whoever humbles*
> *himself like this child is the greatest in the*
> *kingdom of heaven.*
> *Matthew 18:1-4*

what is precious

The single most overwhelming sentiment I brought back from my semester in Pietermaritzburg, South Africa was a prayer that became my life's song:

> Take what is worthless,
> and make precious my heart.

It is the idea that we were made for precious things, and worthless things just won't do. I saw it every day in South Africa, as a thousand things that would have mattered to me in the States just didn't matter when I was living out of a suitcase with one pair of jeans and one sweatshirt, next door to a game reserve with zebras and down the road from both mansions and impoverished townships. It was easy to tell a worthless thing from a precious thing for a while. I came back to my college campus, where the greatest inconvenience I ever encountered was a line at the coffee shop before class, and my heart was craving the precious things.

It's like premium fuel in a premium car or water to quench our thirst. Our bodies are made up of seventy-five percent[1] water when we are born. I'm not a scientist, but I'm convinced that this is why nothing does the trick in quenching our thirst like water. Our water-based bodies crave that of which they are made. So it is with our hearts and the precious things.

These don't come as easily as water, however, in this day and age and in this human state. They take pruning and refining and sacrificing. We empty our hands to receive more. We prune our branches to bear fruit. We clear worthless things out of the way so that we can risk it all on precious things. We sell our fields to buy the one with the pearl. It is risky business. It is costly business. And it is always-keeping-you-on-your-toes business. It takes sacrifice, availability, and willingness, but it is adventure, freedom, and exhilaration. And it is thirst-quenching.

We are children of the Most Precious Thing, and because of that, we are ruined for anything else. So we seek not what is worthless, what is empty and futile, but what is precious and pure, what is lovely and true, what is noble and praiseworthy. These are the things the Lord breathes and for which our hearts were made.

---

[1] Krulwich, Robert. "Born Wet, Human Babies Are 75 Percent Water. Then Comes The Drying." *NPR*, 26 Nov. 2013, https://www.npr.org/sections/krulwich/2013/11/25/247212488/born-wet-human-babies-are-75-percent-water-then-comes-drying.

Therefore thus says the LORD: "If you return, I will restore you, and you shall stand before me. If you utter what is precious, and not what is worthless, you shall be as my mouth."
Jeremiah 15:19

Finally, brothers, whatever is true, whatever is honorable, whatever is just, whatever is pure, whatever is lovely, whatever is commendable, if there is any excellence, if there is anything worthy of praise, think about these things. What you have learned and received and heard and seen in me—practice these things, and the God of peace will be with you.
Philippians 4:8-9

The kingdom of heaven is like treasure hidden in a field, which a man found and covered up. Then in his joy he goes and sells all that he has and buys that field.
Matthew 13:44

Therefore, if anyone cleanses himself from what is dishonorable, he will be a vessel for honorable use, set apart as holy, useful to the master of the house, ready for every good work.
2 Timothy 2:21

*If then you have been raised with Christ,
seek the things that are above, where Christ
is, seated at the right hand of God. Set your
minds on things that are above, not on
things that are on earth. For you have died,
and your life is hidden with Christ in
God. When Christ who is your life appears,
then you also will appear with him in glory.*
Colossians 3:1-4

cupcakes & pizookies

Of all the things that pass through our memories, there are some that take their shoes off and stay. One of the memories that will never leave me is the first time I ate at a BJ's restaurant. I was dead set on going to the bakery across the street for a cupcake after dinner, and my friend said, "We totally can, but we have to order a pizookie."

"What in the world is a pizookie?"

"A warm, slightly undercooked cookie with a scoop of ice cream on top," she said.

"Okay, we'll have a pizookie, and then we'll get a cupcake."

We never got a cupcake. Instead we laughed about how badly I wanted a cupcake when I had no idea there were pizookies out there in the world. It's the same way I felt about eating bougatsa, souvlaki, and pad thai—left saying, "How in the world was this not a part of my life before, and can we please never go back to life without it again?"

We know what we know. I know that cupcakes are good. But one bite of pizookie and I don't ever want to go back to not knowing about pizookies. I think it's hard for us to grasp Jesus and His treasure because we have no way of understanding it without taking a bite. It's unlike anything we've ever known. And until we know, I imagine Jesus saying, "Oh, my sweet, you have no idea what you're missing." To the rich young ruler, "Frankly, my boy, you won't give two figs about all of this if you just let me show you what I have. Come with me. Be with me for the next three years, and I'll show you." But it's not riches or pleasures or blessings like we've known. It's something else entirely. It's—it's something words could never do justice.

It's Him.

It's not, "Come with me, and I'll show you what to do." It's, "Come with me, and I'll show you who I am." And also, "You're going to love this." The rich young ruler walked away without the treasure because he couldn't bring himself to part with what he knew was good, but I am convinced that if he had gone with Jesus, like taking a bite of a pizookie, he would never go back to life without Him again.

Fear not, little flock, for it is your Father's good pleasure to give you the kingdom. Sell your possessions, and give to the needy. Provide yourselves with moneybags that do not grow old, with a treasure in the heavens that does not fail, where no thief approaches and no moth destroys. For where your treasure is, there will your heart be also.
Luke 12:32-34

But, as it is written, "What no eye has seen, nor ear heard, nor the heart of man imagined, what God has prepared for those who love him"— these things God has revealed to us through the Spirit. For the Spirit searches everything, even the depths of God. For who knows a person's thoughts except the spirit of that person, which is in him? So also no one comprehends the thoughts of God except the Spirit of God. Now we have received not the spirit of the world, but the Spirit who is from God, that we might understand the things freely given us by God. And we impart this in words not taught by human wisdom but taught by the Spirit, interpreting spiritual truths to those who are spiritual.
1 Corinthians 2:9-13

grocery shopping in good company

Things changed the day I realized Jesus wants to go grocery shopping with me. I grew up knowing that Jesus heard my prayers, but my day-to-day was about doing things to serve Him. That's all over the book, isn't it? Serving, following, bringing Him glory. Do this; don't do that; be like Jesus. So I tried to live every day for Jesus, which, please hear me, is not a shameful thing. But things changed when I realized Jesus wants me to live every day with Him. Not just for Him, but with Him. And living with Jesus trumps living for Him because when we engage with Him, we know Him better, and we bear more and more of His heart. We aren't just serving the God of the universe; we are serving with Him, who calls us friends.

In human relationships, we do things for others out of love for them with the love we have received from Christ. We respectfully obey our parents or we surprise a spouse with a gift or an act of service because we love them. But our parents and our spouses don't live inside of us. We operate separately from them, though we can come together. But we have an unfathomable communion with our God, who wanted to be with His people to the extent that He decided to dwell in us at all times.

He put on human flesh and imparted His Holy Spirit because He wanted to be with us—deeply, constantly with us, in every breathing moment we have. And instead of burning bushes and tabernacles and sacrifices on altars, we now get to know and remember at any second of the day that He is ours and that He wants to keep us company in whatever we're doing. Driving in the car, running errands, taking a nap, gathering with friends or with strangers—Jesus is there, doing them with us, keeping us company.

I want to know Jesus, this God who dwells with me always, the One who put on flesh to do every second beside me. I want to hear the rhythm of His heartbeat as the sun rises to its place. I want to know His favorite things and the smile that dances on His face. I don't want to know the future or the roadmap that I should take, but I want to know His heart—the way it moves and the way it breaks. I don't want to know His strategy or His next move; I want to know His fingerprint, so that I'll recognize it when I see its grooves. I want to grocery shop with Him. I want to do everything I possibly can with Him, so that I know Him the way He knows me—intimately and indubitably and constantly. I want to know Him with Whom I am keeping company, because He's the best company that I have ever known.

In that day you will know that I am in my
Father, and you in me, and I in you.
John 14:20

*By this we know that we abide in him and
he in us, because he has given us of his
Spirit. And we have seen and testify
that the Father has sent his Son to be the
Savior of the world. Whoever confesses that
Jesus is the Son of God, God abides in him,
and he in God.*
1 John 4:13

*...the mystery hidden for ages and
generations but now revealed to his
saints. To them God chose to make known
how great among the Gentiles are the
riches of the glory of this mystery, which is
Christ in you, the hope of glory. Him we
proclaim, warning everyone and teaching
everyone with all wisdom, that we may
present everyone mature in Christ. For
this I toil, struggling with all his energy
that he powerfully works within me.*
Colossians 1:26-29

*For this reason I bow my knees before the
Father, from whom every family in heaven
and on earth is named, that according
to the riches of his glory he may grant you
to be strengthened with power through his
Spirit in your inner being, so that Christ
may dwell in your hearts through faith...*
Ephesians 3:14-17

He who doesn't change the subject

I used to think God probably got sick and tired of having the same conversation with me over and over again. I used to think He would be listening to me and thinking to Himself, "There are a million things I want to talk to you about, and you want to keep going over *this*? When are you ever going to move past this?" I used to feel guilty bringing up my desires over and over again because clearly I was missing something, not understanding, or falling behind. But I've learned that Jesus isn't like that. Jesus would talk with us about anything for hours as long as we're having a conversation. He would work through a million questions as long as we're asking and listen for a thousand years as long as there's more we want to talk about because He longs for us to know Him better.

Jesus is a listener, and He's a whisperer, too. There are prayers that I am downright embarrassed about, but I cringe to think about where I would be if I hadn't kept talking to Jesus about those things, over and over again—if I'd have stopped asking or wrestling with His thoughts and mine. Jesus is a wrestler. He doesn't give up on anything, not even a conversation topic. He listens to us struggle to understand His ways, and with grace upon grace, He rolls up His sleeves and says, "Okay, you and Me, until the end. We're going to keep kneading this all the way through until the bubbles and pockets are gone."

No matter how many times we ask the same question, He responds. And not begrudgingly or obligatorily—no, I think He's delighted to work His gospel through our hearts until they look infinitely more like His. And if that work starts with our futile, small, and sometimes downright embarrassing desires, then that's the best conversation topic we could be on because He won't change the subject until He has worked His way through our hearts.

Likewise the Spirit helps us in our weakness. For we do not know what to pray for as we ought, but the Spirit himself intercedes for us with groanings too deep for words. And he who searches hearts knows what is the mind of the Spirit, because the Spirit intercedes for the saints according to the will of God.
Romans 8:26-27

If any of you lacks wisdom, let him ask God, who gives generously to all without reproach, and it will be given him.
James 1:5

truth or dare with Jesus

We were talking about plans and the future and not knowing our next steps, as six young women facing marriage proposals, college graduations and part-time transitional jobs, when one of my fellow young women jokingly said, "Let's play truth or dare, God." My heart laughed and sank at the same time. How many times do we treat God like we're playing truth or dare—urging for Him to spill a secret or daring Him to make a move that makes sense of where we are? It's easy to feel like the ball is in His court and we need Him to do something with it, or if we're holding it in our hands, then we need Him to tell us where to throw it. And it is easy to feel as though every decision, every move, every next step carries the weight of the world.

Often times, I am deeply afraid of being wrong. I am afraid of veering off course and being made a fool by the time I realize it. I hate those moments—the almosts, the plan Bs, and the changed-minds. But after quite a few of them—after I "almost" moved to a foreign country and "almost" became a missionary, I think I've stopped being afraid of almost. I look back on all the things on this journey with Jesus that I would have missed had we taken a different course, and the deepest parts of my heart are overwhelmingly grateful for almost. And most of all, I am grateful that no almost is a surprise or a misstep to the Lord.

I don't think Jesus is waiting for us to uncover some predetermined path before us, though we sometimes make it our lifelong mission to figure out the steps we should take. I don't think He is a distant God, looking down from Heaven saying, "Do this; go here; good, you understand my plan." I don't think He's a puppeteer or a chess player with some illusive strategy we surrender to lifelessly. When we ask for wisdom in decisions, I don't think it works like a password to unlock His future plans for us, so He can then impart His knowledge. I think wisdom is knowing His heart, knowing His ways, and it only comes from knowing Him and stepping with Him side by side in life. Have you noticed that Scripture doesn't come with life plans and step one-two-threes, but it is filled to the brim with Jesus—the Word—and the heart of God? He's not jumping down from Heaven to give us His answers; He's jumping down from Heaven to give us Himself.

I think that when we reach a fork in the road, He just wants to go with us and walk with us, side by side, every step of the way, wherever it leads. He wants to give us life along the way and tune our hearts to His as we step to His rhythm. Because the truth is, whatever road we walk with Jesus is going to be the right road, and anywhere with Jesus is where we are supposed to be—just *with* Jesus, getting to know His heart.

*...that the God of our Lord Jesus Christ, the
Father of glory, may give you the Spirit of
wisdom and of revelation in the knowledge
of him...*
Ephesians 1:17

the punctuation of Jesus

I used to ask the Lord to emphasize the things He's trying to tell me so that I don't miss them. I would say, "Lord, you know me; I'm going to miss it if you don't say it loudly. So whatever you want me to know, use the bold letters and a few exclamation points." But I don't think Jesus is really like that. He doesn't come in with a drum, announcing Himself, and He's not really a mic-dropper, though He'd have every reason to be. He came as a baby and told the healed not to tell of whom they had met because He came to serve, not to be served—not really exclamation point living.

When I think about the most mind-blowing things Jesus has done in this story of ours, they always start simply and rather subtly. They don't start with exclamation points. Jesus is a disrupter, it's true, and He stops me in my tracks, but He moves in slower rhythms than I do. His is a gentle pace. He's never hurried or afraid of running out of time like I am. His ways are understated, and His moves start small and ripple. So much of my story with Jesus has been whispered, and a notion that starts an inch above the ground grows to bigger than I can fathom. That's Jesus—I think He uses a lot of ellipses. He lets even the most glorious of epiphanies sink in slowly... like they should.

So I don't ask Jesus to use exclamation points anymore. His ways are smaller, yet much more ample and well-supplied than I think they are, but no matter how quiet His whispers or understated His moves, He lets them grow.

> *And behold, the LORD passed by, and a*
> *great and strong wind tore the mountains*
> *and broke in pieces the rocks before*
> *the LORD, but the LORD was not in the wind.*
> *And after the wind an earthquake, but*
> *the LORD was not in the earthquake. And*
> *after the earthquake a fire, but*
> *the LORD was not in the fire. And after the*
> *fire the sound of a low whisper.*
> *1 Kings 19:11-12*

> *But whoever would be great among you*
> *must be your servant, and whoever would*
> *be first among you must be your slave, even*
> *as the Son of Man came not to be served*
> *but to serve, and to give his life*
> *as a ransom for many.*
> *Matthew 20:26-28*

a chair for standing

I was looking for a small accent chair for the corner of my room. I didn't want it to take up a lot of space; I wanted to be able to move it so that I could easily use it as a step stool to reach my bookshelf; and I wanted it to have a unique personality about it. I found a photo online of a chair at an estate sale nearby and fell in love with it instantly. It was a small vanity chair with a white leather seat and a dainty metal frame, and to me it was perfect. I could see my handmade pillows and crocheted blankets adorning it beautifully.

As my mom and I drove to the sale the next day, I told her that if it was still there, I wanted it, no matter the cost. We walked into the house, and I found it right away, sitting there as beautifully in person as I imagined, and I let out a gasp and said, "There it is!" When I walked up to it, I heard a woman's voice say, "It's sold." She had put it into her pile of a hundred things she was going to buy, paying way less than I would have been willing to pay for that chair.

As I walked around the rest of the house, completely uninterested in anything but that "sold" chair, I saw another one. It was solid wood, small and moveable, in a medium dark finish. I think I stared at it for a solid ninety seconds because I wasn't sure how I felt about it. Deep into my decision-making staring session, a gentleman, who apparently had been watching me try to figure out if I liked it, said, "It fits you perfectly." I laughed and said, "You think so?" And then I sat in it.

He was right; it did fit me perfectly. Though I had thought that solid wood wouldn't be as comfortable as padded leather, I was wrong. The chair curved around my back perfectly, and it felt like a little place of my own—like a blanket fort, it felt like something I could escape in. It was solid as a rock and much stronger and sturdier than that white vanity chair I was swooning over, which I probably wouldn't have been able to stand on to reach my bookshelf without being wobbly and unsafe. Ironically, when the woman who was buying my white vanity chair stood up, I saw that she was sitting in the unsold wooden chair's twin because even she knew that the wood chair was better for sitting.

I wanted that white chair because it was beautiful, but it wasn't the chair I needed. This solid wood brown chair was. It wasn't what I was looking for, but it fit right and fulfilled the strong and steady purpose for which I needed it. Jesus' gifts are like that. Sometimes they aren't as appealing to us as our own desires, but they are solid and built for helping us stand, while also wrapping around us safely and securely as we rest. His ways are stronger and sturdier than ours, and their purpose fulfills more than we are usually willing to settle for. And even though they don't always catch our eye, His desires for us are better than the chairs that sit daintily in corners of rooms. His gifts are the chairs for standing, solid and trustworthy and safe, just like He is.

He only is my rock and my salvation, my fortress; I shall not be shaken. On God rests my salvation and my glory; my mighty rock, my refuge is God.
Psalm 62:6-7

For as the heavens are higher than the earth, so are my ways higher than your ways and my thoughts than your thoughts. For as the rain and the snow come down from heaven and do not return there but water the earth, making it bring forth and sprout, giving seed to the sower and bread to the eater, so shall my word be that goes out from my mouth; it shall not return to me empty, but it shall accomplish that which I purpose, and shall succeed in the thing for which I sent it.
Isaiah 55:9-11

the time we gave up awkward for lent

I said it half-jokingly: "We should give up awkward for lent." We had been talking about how much we admire the people who are so comfortable with others that they just never feel awkward, and because of it, you feel comfortable with them, too—as if nothing you said or did would be unaccepted or perceived as awkward. You know who I am talking about? The ones who are just always themselves, and they allow you to be yourself, too. Given that it was the time of year for lent, I jokingly said we should just refuse to feel awkward. My sweet friend laughed, and then about five seconds later, we both had a "wait, actually..." moment, in which the joke became a seriously good idea. "Wait, actually... This could change our lives," she said. I agreed.

The months that followed were incredibly rich with so much more than just not feeling awkward. We met ourselves. We discovered how deeply we all long to be known. It started with giving ourselves grace in the small instances we would normally say, "Oh gosh, that was awkward. Why did I say that?" or "Why didn't I say that?" Anytime one of us would use the word "awkward," which was rather frequent for us tend-to-be-shy introverts, the other would say, "No. We don't believe in awkward." And it grew to discovering who we are and how beautifully and uniquely the Lord created our little hearts with their own rhythms and favorite dance moves. We learned more about loving the Jesus who is never embarrassed by us, who doesn't think we're awkward, and who likes it when we are who He created us to be in Him.

One of the most awkward feelings I know in this life surfaces when I'm dancing in front of others. I can dance the heck out of a kitchen with a meal in the making and a song turned up loud, but in front of others, all I feel is awkward. But here's what I've learned about the best dancers—they are the ones who don't care, who are unrestrained. They are the ones who are just themselves. Dancing is less about moves than it is about freedom. The people with the best moves are the ones who know they're free and dance like it. And they're the ones who make others feel welcome to dance freely too.

I think it's the same with being ourselves in this kingdom—just like good dancers, you can trust people who are themselves, who tell the truth about themselves without fear of how it will be received. The people in my life who inspire me the most are the ones who know who they are in Christ, live in that freedom, and invite others into that freedom as well. The ones who know they are fully known and loved by God, and that they don't have to make themselves worthy. They can dance freely.

These people remind me of Christ—Jesus broke all kinds of social norms in ways that would be perceived as awkward. He talked to prostitutes, ate with tax collectors, touched lepers. I bet everywhere He went, people were like, "Ummm, this is so awkward." But I don't think Jesus believes in awkward. He's a come-as-you-are, no-masks-allowed, authenticity-only kind of God when it comes to relationships.

We got to know this Jesus better when we, too, refused to believe in awkward, and we found that the grace we gave ourselves, like the best dancers, extended to others, too. As we suspected, it did change our lives and all of our social interactions, forever.

Friends, may we dance outside of our kitchens and give up awkward for good. May we find the courage to be the first ones to be ourselves, fully known and loved by Christ, and may others be free to find that courage in our presence as well.

Therefore welcome one another as Christ
has welcomed you, for the glory of God.
Romans 15:7

I am the good shepherd. I know my own
and my own know me, just as the Father
knows me and I know the Father
John 10:14-15

you who can't ice skate

He asked me if I liked ice skating. I said no.

He said I was going to be a speed skater. He said I'd do powerful things for the kingdom. But I didn't feel like a speed skater. I felt like a butterfly or something fragile, not a speed skater. And quite frankly, nothing about speed skating was of any interest to me. I basically dismissed what the pastor of that twelve-person congregation in Pietermaritzburg, South Africa told me because of how much I dislike ice skating.

Eight months later, I was reminded of this interaction and started thinking about why I hate ice skating so much. I don't like ice skating because I'm not good at it. My ankles are too tiny; my balance is too unsteady; my body wasn't made for ice skating. And eight months later, it dawned on me that the pastor's question wasn't a mistake.

This time, I laughed. I laughed the way I only do when Jesus does something I can't believe. And I went back to that moment, only I imagined Jesus asking the question and then going on to say, "You know those things you think you can't do? Those things you don't feel good enough or equipped to do? You're not just going to do them; you're going to do them with power—*My* power. With swift, fearless power. You, my dear, who can't ice skate, are going to be a speed skater."

That's just like Jesus, isn't it? To do those things with us we think we could never do and to call us what we never thought we could be? God had a similar conversation with Moses. And Moses' response was much like mine—I'm not a speed skater; I can't even ice skate. Only it was, *"Who am I that I should go to Pharaoh and bring the children of Israel out of Egypt?" (Exodus 3:11)*, and, *"Oh, my Lord, I am not eloquent, either in the past or since you have spoken to your servant, but I am slow of speech and of tongue" (Exodus 4:10).*

Moses had murdered an Egyptian in Chapter 2, and Jesus is all, "We're going to speed skate." And Moses says, "I can't ice skate." And the Lord says, "We, Moses, *We.*"

He said, "But I will be with you..." God said to Moses, "I AM WHO I AM." And he said, "Say this to the people of Israel: 'I AM has sent me to you'" (Exodus 3:12, v. 14).

Then the LORD said to him, "Who has made man's mouth? Who makes him mute, or deaf, or seeing, or blind? Is it not I, the LORD? Now therefore go, and I will be with your mouth and teach you what you shall speak" (Exodus 4:11-12).

"You who can't ice skate are going to speed skate, my dear, but it is I, I AM WHO I AM, who will be with you." I should have known. But it's also just like Jesus to let it click eight months later.

But we have this treasure in jars of clay, to show that the surpassing power belongs to God and not to us.
2 Corinthians 4:7

the story the Creator intends

In the sixth season of my favorite television series, contract negotiations led the creator to leave the show. It couldn't survive without her. The new writers ruined it by episode three of the next season. The plot moved all over the place faster than a fly escaping a swatter, and the actors refused to continue the show without the creator. Nine years later, Netflix made a deal with the creator to give the ending she always wanted—the one she intended from its creation with the last four words she planned years before she left. Her ending, the one the show was created for, quite frankly, was painful. It was difficult and uncomfortable to watch, it was shocking and disillusioning, and it was more "What in the world?" than happily ever after. But it was beautiful. It was a tragically beautiful doozy of a something. It left all the ends untied. People were expecting an ending. A this-person-ends-up-with-that-person and they're all on their way to amen, but instead it was messy and complicated and completely undone. And it was perfect. It was richer and deeper and far more artful than I could have predicted. The feel-gooders were outraged. But the story, which ended on the cliffhanger of cliffhangers was exactly the message the creator wanted to say, with extra layers of depth and intention.

The gospel, our Creator's story, is kind of like that. It's far from feel-good, and it's hard to swallow. You have to wrestle with it more than a few times before you fully appreciate its intricacies. Flesh has to wrestle with Spirit before it understands that what the Creator intends is the only thing that truly satisfies. It's the only ending that truly does justice to the beginning and middle. It doesn't make sense to our intuition or reason, it goes against our natural proclivities, and it's unconventional, but the story the Creator has in mind is so much richer and deeper and more beautiful, though tragically, than the feel-good one we come up with. When He takes it where He always wanted it to go, the result is striking and jaw-dropping and silence-inducing, and it says everything that needs to be said.

Creator pours all of His heart into His good, good creation, who turn their back on Him time and again. Though they don't grasp the glory of Him who made them, He keeps pursing them endlessly, giving up His life in their place. Some of them come to know His truth, His grace, and His love, and their hearts are freed, though they have to wrestle every day to walk in that freedom and remember that they are no longer enslaved to death. Creator wins His good creation, His portion, His inheritance, and still, others die anyway.

I told you, it's more, "What in the world?" than anything else when you think about it. Even as I write a shortened version of my understanding of it, I can't do justice to the story the Creator intends—the tragically beautiful doozy of a something.

For the desires of the flesh are against the
Spirit, and the desires of the Spirit
are against the flesh...
Galatians 5:17

...but whoever drinks of the water that I
will give him will never be thirsty again.
The water that I will give him will
become in him a spring of water
welling up to eternal life.
John 4:14

But we impart a secret and hidden wisdom
of God, which God decreed before the ages
for our glory. None of the rulers of this age
understood this, for if they had, they would
not have crucified the Lord of glory. But, as
it is written, "What no eye has seen, nor ear
heard, nor the heart of man imagined,
what God has prepared for those who love
him"—these things God has revealed to us
through the Spirit.
1 Corinthians 2:7-10

take a seat

As I was boarding the plane, I passed by a little boy about two feet tall standing in between the seats with his face to the window. All of a sudden, his face lit up with excitement, and he grabbed his dad's arm shouting, "Daddy! Daddy! I see an airplane!" Dad said, with a laugh and almost as much excitement as his little boy, "Buddy! You're on an airplane right now!"

Life is like that sometimes. Sometimes we see airplanes, and our eyes or our hearts fill with admiration, and we don't realize we're on an airplane of our own. Sometimes we watch other people's adventures, and we forget to take a seat in ours.

Maybe this little boy had never seen an airplane that close, or maybe he just loves them enough that seeing one out the window at an airport seemed like a big deal, but he was silent after Dad said he was on an airplane. I don't think he really got it. It probably didn't look like what he thought an airplane looks like on the inside. I could see the confused little "What?" on his face as he grappled with this thought.

I am this little boy sometimes, admiring other people's stories, which look different on the outside than the inside of mine. And I wonder how many times Jesus wants to say, "Just wait, little one. This thing we're on right now—it takes off. We're going to go somewhere from right inside this airplane. So let's get in our seats and buckle up. You'll see."

I wonder how many times Jesus just wants us to take our seat in His kingdom—the one He intended for us. When we're asking Him what we should do and what's going on and why and where and when and how, I imagine Him saying, "Take your seat, little one. You'll see."

> *But God, being rich in mercy, because*
> *of the great love with which he loved*
> *us, even when we were dead in our*
> *trespasses, made us alive together with*
> *Christ—by grace you have been saved—and*
> *raised us up with him and seated us with*
> *him in the heavenly places in Christ Jesus...*
> *Ephesians 2:4-6*

socks & bare feet

My college roommate always made fun of me for coming home from class and changing into my pajamas at three o'clock in the afternoon. She'd say, "Really? You're done for the day?" I always explained to her that I would just change back into clothes if I needed to leave or if someone came over, but while I'm home, I want to be comfortable. There are pros and cons to my homebody nature, but one of my favorite things in the world is taking my shoes off when I walk in the door. It is the most freeing reminder that we're here now; we'll be staying awhile; and I've taken my shoes off—I'm not about to leave. With my shoes off, I always feel like making art. I never make things with my shoes on. Songs, paintings, handwritten stories, blankets, dance parties—all of those are made in socks or bare feet.

That's life with Jesus. It's coming home and being here, now. It's socks and bare feet. No matter how different every season is, it's Jesus saying, "I know we've never been here before, but my, my, are we going to be here deeply. Go ahead, make yourself at home in Me. Hang the tapestry on the wall, put up the lights you like. Sure, we can have more pillows. And more tears—that's okay, too. We can talk about the world and the mess and the things we don't know enough about. We can talk about the things that hurt, the things that heal, and the things that do both. We can stay up all night. And we can also go to sleep early. We can create and we can linger; we can forgo clocks and shoes. This is ours. You and me, yours and mine. Here, now. In our socks and bare feet."

> *Jesus answered him, "If anyone loves me,*
> *he will keep my word, and my Father will*
> *love him, and we will come to him*
> *and make our home with him."*
> *John 14:23*

turns out, we'll never have it together

The months following my college graduation were disillusioning. It was a season of life that didn't follow the growing up playbook I imagined as a child. Life was smaller, slower paced, and seemingly anticlimactic. Simple things felt impossible. Amidst the unexplainable tears and repeatedly forgetting to fill my gas tank, I realized that though I am still new to "adulthood," I don't think adults have ever had it together. We children just always thought they did. Honestly, I think we're all mostly just winging it.

I used to think David the giant-slayer, adulterer, psalmist was an extreme. There was this silent notion in my mind that the rest of us don't have to be like David or any of the faith patriarchs who knew the Lord and didn't choose Him all the time. I genuinely thought it was possible for us to be giant-slayer and psalmist and never forget who we are. But God's very best—the gospel narrators and supporting roles—were always in shambles.

Here's why I think they, and we, are always in shambles, never having it together: having it all figured out, keeping it all together, is something only God can do. It's something only our infinite, incomprehensible Creator of the universe, almighty and sovereign Lord of lords can do. And if we somehow think we can do it, we are equating ourselves with God. No, we can never expect to have it all together. The most we can do is be in pieces with Jesus. And the God of pieced-together Goliath and Bathsheba Davids will hold our hearts like newborn things.

In becoming more acquainted with the adults I used to think had it all together but really don't, I have found that the wisest ones know how to not have it figured out, how to not be in control, how to be held in pieces by Jesus. They know that the new creations they are in Christ are not self-sufficient and ripened, even in their adulthood, but that the God who pieces us together holds our hearts accordingly, like fragile, precious, newborn things. And needing this God to hold us together is the very best position we could be in because He is faithful to nurture and sustain us and because everyone else needs Him, too.

> *...all things were created through him and for him. And he is before all things, and in him all things hold together.*
> *Colossians 1:16-17*

> *Therefore, if anyone is in Christ, he is a new creation. The old has passed away; behold, the new has come. All this is from God, who through Christ reconciled us to himself and gave us the ministry of reconciliation...*
> *2 Corinthians 5:17-18*

come closer

You know those times when it has been forever—I mean, way too embarrassingly and inexcusably long—since we've talked to Jesus? It gets to the point where we don't even know how to start the conversation anymore, so we just keep putting it off. It's unbelievable how hard it seems, isn't it? It happens with friendships sometimes, too. It's so much easier to keep in touch when you're already in touch. When months have passed since you've talked to someone, it becomes like, "Well, what difference does another month make?"

Sometimes I don't want to start the conversation with Jesus again because I know it will have to start with an apology—I can't in good conscience talk to the Lord without acknowledging that we haven't been talking. When it happens in friendship, though, and I am finally reunited with someone after a long absence, I never feel that same need to apologize or explain myself. A dear friend has never said, "Where have you been? How dare you not talk to me?" Usually, I am greeted by, "How are you? It's been forever. Catch me up. It's so good to see you." Because when I miss people I care about, all I want to do is talk to them—I don't tend to care about lording the absence over their heads, as if an explanation is the prerequisite for a conversation with me.

I think the Lord, though He'd have every right to be upset with our wandering hearts, feels the same way about us—He misses His beloved ones, and all He wants to do is catch up. When we seek His face again, I think He's just bursting with, "It is good to see you," and, "Hallelujah, you're home." He never wishes shame on His little sheep; He just wants them near always. When I feel unworthy and I distance myself, like a punishment of sorts, all He has ever wanted me to do is come closer. No prerequisites, no earning His good graces, just "Come closer. Catch me up. How's your heart? Not good, right? I know; I missed you, too. Come closer. " He is a God missing His friend, as mind-blowing as it is that He calls us friends, and all He wants is to talk to us—to call us up in the middle of the night, hear about our day, and tell us about His. He's less concerned with where we've been than where we are now, and once we're here, He doesn't want us to distance ourselves anymore—all He longs for is that we come closer.

... but I have called you friends, for all that I
have heard from my Father I have made
known to you.
John 15:15

Draw near to God, and he will draw
near to you.
James 4:8

...if my people who are called by my name humble themselves, and pray and seek my face and turn from their wicked ways, then I will hear from heaven and will forgive their sin and heal their land.
2 Chronicles 7:14

What man of you, having a hundred sheep, if he has lost one of them, does not leave the ninety-nine in the open country, and go after the one that is lost, until he finds it? And when he has found it, he lays it on his shoulders, rejoicing. And when he comes home, he calls together his friends and his neighbors, saying to them, 'Rejoice with me, for I have found my sheep that was lost.'
Luke 15:4-6

whiplash & panic attacks

I had been mentally preparing myself for the world's highest commercial bridge bungee jump for months. I kept thinking if I could just get myself off the bridge, I'd be home free. I had been warned not to tense up my muscles because that's how people get whiplash doing this sort of thing. But I never imagined what falling would feel like on my face or in my stomach or on every millimeter of my body pushing through the air un-surrounded by any barrier other than my clothing. The moment my feet left the edge, panic took over before I even had a second to think about it. I inadvertently tensed up, my body folded in half on the first bounce of the bungee cord, people thought I kicked my face (because that's what it looked like), and I did get whiplash.

A similar thing happened when we went shark cage diving a few weeks later. Once in the cage, after struggling to figure out how to hook my feet under the bar that holds them in place and accidentally kicking the people next to me, I experienced my first ever panic attack and felt like I couldn't breathe.

The truth about my bungee jump and my shark cage dive is that I messed them up. These incredibly daring, once-in-a-lifetime, while-in-South-Africa things were supposed to earn me cool mom points with my kids one day, and I was the epitome of uncool. My body told on me. I couldn't fool anyone once I kicked my face and stopped being able to breathe. Everyone around me found out what happens when you throw me off a bridge or in a cage near sharks—I get whiplash and a panic attack.

But truthfully, I wish my messiness told on me more often—maybe not so literally, but I think it's good for the soul to be exposed sometimes—to be embraced by the honesty of our messiness. Not one person thought I was insane for panicking over sharks and a 700-foot bridge. I kind of wish the rest of life was like that—understanding and giving grace for people, considering the sharks or the bridges they've seen lately. Because my, my, am I glad that it's okay to be a mess in this life—that it's even some kind of inevitable, and that we still get to be a part of the adventure though we lose our cool in the middle of it.

I don't think Jesus minds that we're ungraceful adventure buddies—that we do the jump wrong or can't find where to put our feet. If He did, none of us would be on the adventure at all. He knows with whom He's jumping off the bridge or into cages near sharks, and He wants us to do it with Him anyway. He wants to be there with us, suspended in the air at the bottom of the canyon, hanging by our feet while all the blood rushes to our heads and we see the world upside down for a long minute. He wants to be there clutching the top of the cage for dear life, even though you shouldn't put your hands there, when we see the shark's eyes a short yard away from our own. He wants to be in every panic-filled, far-from-graceful, un-composed moment of the greatest adventure with Him. And in the end, when we come up from the canyon and the water, double-checking to see that we're still breathing, and all we tell Instagram is that we made it, He doesn't say anything about the whiplash and the panic attack either. He's not thinking He wasted an adventure on a mess of an adventure buddy. He's thinking, "Let's do it again."

For by grace you have been saved through
faith. And this is not your own doing; it is
the gift of God, not a result of works,
so that no one may boast.
Ephesians 2:8-9

The steadfast love of the LORD never ceases;
his mercies never come to an end;
they are new every morning;
great is your faithfulness.
Lamentations 3:22-23

right on time

I played at a lot of open mic nights in college. They were some of my favorite memories from those four years, and one of the most memorable was an event to raise support for a social justice cause. I didn't have any strictly social justice themed songs, so I wrote one the day before. Before I started, I said, "I wrote this song yesterday. It doesn't have a name yet, and my mom hasn't heard it, so it could totally be an epic fail, but try to be forgiving, and my hope with this is that we won't stand still." Two-thirds through the song, in my favorite part of the bridge, my voice cracked, and I forgot the words. So I broke the rules of performing, and I stopped playing. I said, "Alright, let's try this again because that's my favorite part of the song." Then, as if the voice cracking and words forgetting wasn't enough, I couldn't find my place to come in with the chords, and I had a few more false starts, a.k.a. this perfectionist's worst nightmare.

Sometimes in this walk with Jesus, there are redos and false starts. And when they happen—when we get weary and our voices crack or we lose our place and forget the words, He gives us a minute. He lets us take a breath, remember our place, and try again. And no matter how many times it takes us to remember and let it stick, no matter how many missteps until we find our place, He greets us with, "You're right on time," just as the open mic audience was gracious with me until I managed to finish the song. While we are thinking we should have been here ages ago, I think God is just bursting with gladness that we made it. That we took a minute, remembered our place in the song, and finished it. Right on time.

Fight the good fight of the faith. Take hold
of the eternal life to which you were called
and about which you made the good
confession in the presence of
many witnesses.
1 Timothy 6:12

I press on toward the goal for the prize of
the upward call of God in Christ Jesus.
Philippians 3:14

He who cut wood

I wish I had a count of how many times in my life I've been asked what I want to do when I grow up. From my dress-up days to post bachelor's degree, the search for "what I'm going to do" with my future has sometimes felt impossibly burdensome—not because I don't have dreams, but because I do, and it takes time to grow into them. Many days, I feel too small, like my three-year-old self being asked the question for the first time.

But I think of Jesus. He started His ministry at thirty years old, in an age where people got married and started families at sixteen. There were all these things He was preparing to do, but He had to wait. And He must have known at some point that He was God, but He went to school like everybody else and cut wood like a regular carpenter until He was *thirty*. It must have felt like forever. God in the flesh had years of waiting, preparing, and watching other people start their lives. But I bet He took it all in, gleaned from every day, and learned constantly. I bet He spent a lot of time disciplining Himself for game time.

And I bet He who knows waiting and preparing, dreaming and disciplining, feels the pains of growing and the pains of being too small with us. I bet He sits on the stoop with us at the bottom of the stairs on the night of our college graduation when we're wondering when in the world we're going to grow into our future and says, "I know; I really do. But trust me, we're working on something *good*."

And the Word became flesh and dwelt
among us, and we have seen His glory,
glory as of the only Son from the Father,
full of grace and truth.
John 1:14

why the sun sets

We were sitting on a blanket, staring out into the canyon-esque space where the jagged edges of the mountains meet. The sun was doing its dance before ducking out for the night, and my sweet friend wondered aloud why Jesus made the sun set every day when He didn't have to. Jesus didn't have to make anything, and He made it all, which I deeply hope will eternally blow my mind. But I think Jesus made the sun set to remind us that we're not invincible, that we need rest. I think He made the sun set for the same reason He made water. We need it. We are small and finite, and we run out. We don't always remember that, but I have this small suspicion that they had an easier time remembering it by candlelight, before Edison's thousandth attempt lit up the world.

I think Jesus created us to need water and sunsets to remind us that we need Him. But also, that He delivers. He provides, and He sustains, and He renews. From the mountains and the sun to our finite skin and bones, what He created, He maintains and He makes new every day, without ceasing. And as faithful as the sun is to rise again,

He will be—invincible and constant and the fulfiller of needs.

Therefore, we rest. We rest in knowing that life goes down slowly like wine. The sun sets for our good and rises again just like it should lest we forget that it's okay to have days that are small, bounded, and paced. Because in this life of sunrises and sets, we have infinitely more days with our faithfully good Sustainer.

And he said to them, "The Sabbath was
made for man, not man for the Sabbath."
Mark 2:27

Have you not known? Have you not heard?
The LORD is the everlasting God,
the Creator of the ends of the earth.
He does not faint or grow weary;
his understanding is unsearchable.
Isaiah 40:28

tomorrow is another day

Whenever I was in the middle of creating or thinking or scheming at night as a child, my mom would say, "Tomorrow is another day." She was essentially telling me to go to bed. It was a polite way of nudging me to stop reading or writing or making art and to finish whatever I didn't want to put down tomorrow. I've always needed and hated this reminder. But in the middle of the longest quilting project I've ever tackled, my mom once again gently reminded her twenty something daughter who doesn't adhere to bedtimes anymore that tomorrow is another day, and that time, I heard it differently. After she said it, I looked down at the hundreds of little fabric squares I was slowly making progress on, and I smiled at the thought of waking up to another chance to return to them. As I breathed in that sweet realization, I thought, "Wow, I get to do this again tomorrow. It will be here in the morning, and I get to keep chipping away at it again."

I laugh at how many times I have grumbled at the thought of not being able to finish today's work today. I hate leaving in the middle of a half-created thing. And yet, resting was never meant to be a burden, and tomorrow was never meant to be a dreary thing; it was meant to be a gift— a chance to refresh and return. And in this walk with Jesus, sometimes it feels like we're not doing things quickly enough, like progress is slow, and therefore, we have to finish another day. But when we wake up in the morning, guess Who's there and never in a hurry, so excited to see our sweet, sleepy faces; roll up His sleeves; and go back to making something beautiful, again and again and again. Man, am I thankful that we don't have to finish everything in a day, that we get to keep chipping away at our conversations with Jesus, our questions, and our next steps; and that tomorrow, we get to know more of this God than we did today. Yes, praise Jesus—tomorrow is another day.

Lord, you have been our dwelling place in
all generations. Before the mountains were
brought forth, or ever you had formed the
earth and the world, from everlasting to
everlasting you are God.
Psalm 90:1-2

Unless the LORD builds the house, those
who build it labor in vain. Unless
the LORD watches over the city,
the watchman stays awake in vain.
It is in vain that you rise up early and go
late to rest, eating the bread of anxious toil;
for he gives to his beloved sleep.
Psalm 127:1-2

new things are stirring

I keep three different types of journals at all times, each serving a distinct purpose and telling a different side of the same story. One is a prayer journal—the raw, hash-it-out-with-Jesus-as-life-happens. That's my favorite. Another is filled with words other people wrote or said that I want to remember. It's the one I carry with me wherever Christ-followers gather. The third is the one in which I write one sentence every day. As you can imagine, that one takes the longest to fill. Though I started each of these journals years apart and fill them at different paces, they all recently somehow reached their final pages at the same time. It felt funny and strange and a little unsettling, but it served as a tangible reminder that new things are stirring.

Sometimes it's hard to remember that new things are happening, that the Lord is stirring things in our hearts we've yet to realize, and that He is never idle. Most of life feels like the middle of something—the middle of a task, the middle of a lesson, the middle of a season or a story. And it's not until we look back that we realize that the Lord was doing a dozen things in our hearts at once.

There is never just one thing with Jesus. And sometimes that fact is overwhelming, and sometimes it goes unnoticed, but His works are myriad and abundant. He is a multi-tasker—but not the juggling, distracted kind of multi-tasker we know too well. No, He is a patient one and a skilled one, a thoughtful and calculated one. He knows; He sees; and He tends. He works in the middle of a million things and somehow, in a way we may never fully comprehend, He holds them all together. He never drops the ball, and things never slip through His fingers. He never forgets to finish a story, though sometimes when we're in the middle of it, it can feel that way. And He can also birth new things in the middle of an unfinished story—He can handle that; they can all fit in His steady hands. So in case you can't see it from one day to the next, in the middle of your unfinished stories, rest easy, dear one, new things are stirring, from the most skilled hands that never drop a thing.

Behold, I am doing a new thing; now it
springs forth, do you not perceive it? I will
make a way in the wilderness and
rivers in the desert.
Isaiah 43:19

And he is before all things, and in him all
things hold together.
Colossians 1:17

open bodies of water

I have always been a little bit afraid of swimming in open bodies of water. My swimming teachers told my mom it's because we had a hot tub at home, so I was used to always having walls around me in the water. I loved swimming pools as a child, and I was happy to be in the water, but they said I was always hesitant to go too far from the edge. Even now, I'm wary of going too far out into the ocean or a lake, where there are no walls or anything to grab ahold of.

My senior year of college, I stayed a weekend in a house on a lake with friends I was still starting to get to know. I went canoeing for the first time, and we found out that I don't jump gracefully out of canoes into water like they do, nor do I know how to pull myself back into the canoe when I'm done being afraid to swim too far. Those ladies I had just begun to know became some of my best friends after that weekend, but at the time, man, did I feel vulnerable in that open body of water.

Sometimes loving Jesus feels like that—like there are no boundaries. Like nothing is hidden—a little humiliating. My uncoordinated self can't pretend to be graceful with Him. Jesus knows that when I jump out of a canoe into water, I look like a flying squirrel, and that when I climb back into the canoe, I look like a beached whale. He knows the difference between my having fun laugh and my embarrassed laugh. He knows how ungraceful I can be when I'm trying to do new things and have it all together at the same time.

Loving Jesus is a lot of being out of my element, a lot of doing new things for the first time—talking to strangers, sharing my heart, going places I've never been, and being displaced from my comfort zone time and again. Loving Jesus is also a lot of being reminded that Jesus doesn't care if I look like a flying squirrel or a beached whale. He laughs with me when I'm losing it. He reminds me that everything is going to be okay when I'm freaking out about the fish in the water. He makes me do the things that scare me a little bit, and He makes me glad I did in the end.

And He reminds me, much to my relief, that I don't have to worry about nailing my canoe jumps because I don't have to glorify myself. I glory in Jesus alone, and He has proven Himself to never fail, so His reputation stands. Loving Jesus is simultaneously humiliating and comforting, embarrassing and freeing—like being a hot tub swimmer in an open body of water.

> *Not to us, O LORD, not to us, but to your*
> *name give glory, for the sake of your*
> *steadfast love and your faithfulness!*
> *Psalm 115:1*

good fools

When I was eighteen, I went to a concert in which the lead singer called a guy named AJ up to the stage to sing the lyrics with him. Halfway through explaining how their singing together was going to go, AJ, who was obviously under the influence of something, decided to jump off the stage and go crowd surfing instead. The lead singer stood there a little dumbfounded for a second and said, "That was not the plan, AJ." It became an expression my best friend and I use whenever life decides to go crowd surfing instead of singing the lyrics we taught it.

I have found that the longer I walk with Jesus and the more of Him I come to know in this life, the more it is filled with "that was not the plan, AJ"s. I can count on one hand how many times this walk with Jesus has gone as I expected, led me to where I thought we were going, and looked like exactly what I asked for. And I can't count high enough for the number of times Jesus has given me what I never would have asked for but exactly what I needed. It seems like every season these days is the last place I thought I would be. And I have finally resolved that I can't figure out

God and that His ways will always be different than mine. I am never going to be able to predict His next move; I am just going to know His heart more and more and more, so moving with Him will be my absolute favorite thing, though equally as unpredictable.

Jesus is a God who goes off script. He always has been. Talking to women, touching lepers, eating with tax collectors, being born as a baby, and dying a wrongfully convicted criminal—nowhere near the script. And His script-flipping tends to make a fool out of me. Sometimes I stand there a little dumbfounded like the lead singer watching AJ crowd surf. A little "What in the world?" and a little "That was not the plan, AJ," except unlike AJ, Jesus knows exactly what we're doing. And that's why God's grace makes good fools and being dumbfounded is the best part of adventuring with Him. He keeps flipping the script, and I turn out to be a fool in His grace, but a good fool—the kind He has never failed and never will. The kind He loves too much to leave an unwitting fool, so He points out my foolishness instead. But He never shames me with it—it's more like a surprise. It's more like a, "Guess what? You were so, so wrong. I'm the God of wonder and your heart and all things good, and I've got things you can't even think of up my sleeve. It's going to blow your mind." And it does. Every time.

> *But if it is by grace, it is no longer on the*
> *basis of works; otherwise grace would no*
> *longer be grace.*
> *Romans 11:6*

Oh, the depth of the riches and wisdom and
knowledge of God! How unsearchable
are his judgments and how
Inscrutable his ways!
Romans 11:33

Trust in the LORD with all your heart,
and do not lean on your own
understanding. In all your ways
acknowledge him, and he will make
straight your paths.
Proverbs 3:5-6

Goodness Himself

I've come to the conclusion that the best things in life are also kind of the worst. Even the good, most hopeful things can be near-impossibly hard and the good news requires wrestling. I think that's why Paul tells us not to grow weary in doing good—because in this life, in this flesh, good things can be wearisome. They can be intrusive and arduous. Like honey, they are sweet, but rich and hard to digest without a refining of the palate. They require grace and grit and things that don't come naturally. And the best things we receive in this life will demand the most from us. Have you noticed that? The good things require responsibility, and sometimes their weight is heavy. Marriages take work; children require—*everything*; ministry demands fervent tending and pouring into. You can't take your eyes off of the good things—they have to constantly be cultivated, planted, and sowed in this life, on this side of Heaven. They won't be wearisome in eternity. They may still require work, but the burden won't be heavy; it'll just be good.

But here and now, when we hold even the good things that are wearisome at times, the Jesus who is Goodness Himself is near to us. For He who works things for our good—for that which conforms us to the likeness of Him—is Goodness Himself. And that nearness with He who makes things good is worth every effort in the world. Every wrestling and wearisome moment with Jesus is worth all the good things, hard as they may be.

As for you, brothers, do not grow
weary in doing good.
2 Thessalonians 3:13

And we know that for those who love God
all things work together for good for those
who are called according to his purpose.
For those whom he foreknew he also
predestined to be conformed to the
image of his Son...
Romans 8:28-29

a thousand years to die

I was two months away from walking across the graduation stage, accepting my diploma, and turning the tassel to the rest of my life, and a speaker in senior chapel said something that changed everything for me. She said, "Some of you need to know that when you leave this place and start the rest of your life, you're going into a season. That's all it is, a season."

I don't know a lot about life, but one thing I do know is that it happens in seasons. It doesn't happen careers at a time, or decades, or even life stages at a time. It happens day-by-day, month-by-month, and winter-by-spring-by-summer-by-fall.

Jesus knew that we needed seasons. We needed to break down our lives into smaller segments. And when one segment has worked its life through, there's another one after it to remind us that this story is bigger; this picture is grander. It is greater, and it keeps going, and it never ends. We were made for eternity, but we can't swallow it at once, so we take it one season after another, to remind us that there is life after.

There is life after graduation. There is life after loss; life after leaving; life after whirlwind adventures; life after hardship; life after broken hearts and injustice; life after the things we didn't think we would survive. There is life after changes and "almost" and "This wasn't the plan." This story with Jesus is like a star taking a thousand years to die—it outlives us.

Our seasons that happen one after the other, I have found, get worse and get better, too. Some things get harder and some things get easier when we're not looking. But I am convinced that in the story with Jesus, each chapter is richer than the one before it—rich with challenges, with refinement, with growth, with fullness, and with abundance.

Rich things, like eternity or honey, have to be drizzled or they're a bit overwhelming. We have to grow into them—we don't feed honey to our infants because they can't handle it, and we don't live careers or decades or stages at once because this story outlasts our lives on Earth, like a star taking a thousand years to die.

For everything there is a season, and a time
for every matter under heaven... He
has made everything beautiful in its time.
Also, he has put eternity into man's heart,
yet so that he cannot find out what God has
done from the beginning to the end.
Ecclesiastes 3:1, v. 11

But do not overlook this one fact, beloved, that with the Lord one day is as a thousand years, and a thousand years as one day.
2 Peter 3:8

Your kingdom is an everlasting kingdom, and your dominion endures throughout all generations.
Psalm 145:13

too human again

There are days I just feel too human, days in which there's just something missing, and the commute back to Jesus is longer than usual. I am just as unworthy as I always have been, but some days, it seems less bearable. Some things, some days are just hard.

Jesus is a God who knows that. He's a God who wept for comfort when He didn't have to. He's a God who understands our humanity, and I think He understands loneliness, too. He had a really flawed home team, and I bet He got lonely sometimes. I bet He missed His best friend and needed to encourage Himself sometimes. That's why He prayed in gardens. He doesn't think I'm pathetic for crying in my little bed. Nothing is ever a surprise to Him. He knows that choosing life and love and the precious things is hard. He knows that dancing with Him gets tiring. It doesn't offend Him.

Jesus is never surprised that I'm human. He never forgets, even though it seems like I do. He is a God of every-morning mercy and grace upon grace. And the thing is, grace only does its beautiful best on humans. That is a necessary part of the extraordinary. And when my limbs feel too heavy and my spirit disappointed in me, I imagine that the God of humans says, "I know, little one, but this is how it works. You're human, and I'm yours. From the beginning to the end, I am infinitely yours."

He is a God who came as a human to live among us *always*. And He always has goodness and strength for us, but He comforts us first, before lifting us up again. And He doesn't want us to fake it—He wants us to wrestle and to rest and to lament. But always, He wants to be the place we run to—He wants to be the arms that hold our hearts and the ear that bends down to listen. Always, He just wants to be *with* us, on the good days and bad days, light-on-our-feet days, and dragging-on-the-floor days—because any kind of day with Him is better than a day without Him.

I want that to sink in—enough to be palpable, but still blow my mind. I want to give grace upon grace as I receive it. I want to know deep in my spirit that Jesus loves without restraint, withholding no good thing. I want to behold His always and forever goodness without being surprised that I am fallible. And for as long as I live, I want to feel too human and remember that Jesus is my God.

For the gate is narrow and the way is hard
that leads to life.
Matthew 7:14

*For we do not have a high priest who is
unable to sympathize with our weaknesses,
but one who in every respect has
been tempted as we are, yet without sin. Let
us then with confidence draw near to the
throne of grace, that we may receive mercy
and find grace to help in time of need.*
Hebrews 4:15-16

when you can't get up the mountain

We call it the death hike. We were seventeen and eighteen years old, on our post high school graduation road trip, and my friends, who were all athletes and in good shape, said we were going on a hike. It was a 9-mile out-and-back trail, which I didn't know until we got out of the car and I saw the canyon leading to the mountain I knew I wouldn't be able to climb back up once we got down. I stood at the start of the trail and said, "I don't want to do this. You guys go ahead, and I'll wait here." You can probably guess that they didn't accept that offer, nor did they let me turn around the multiple times that I asked.

Five hours in, it was 105 degrees outside, we were out of water, one friend was wearing another's extra boxers as a bandage around her bleeding knee, one friend was vomiting from dehydration, and my strength had given out. As I suspected, I was not going to be able to make it back up the mountain, despite how close we were to being finished with the trail. While the others forged ahead in their own struggles to the finish, one of my friends stayed behind with me. First, it was for moral support, "You can do this" kind of encouragement, but after a short while, he was literally pushing me up the mountain, leaning his body into my back for the last 45 minutes of the hike. At one point, he asked me how much I weighed to see if he had the strength to carry me instead, but I made it to the top of that mountain with his shoulders pushing me up.

I had never felt more vulnerable. While he used to be my least favorite of the friend group, (it's okay; he knows), through that hike, I gained a deeper appreciation for him than I thought possible. No one else knows what it was like to be pushed up that mountain by him. Conversely, no one else knows what it must have been like for him pouring all of his strength and dedication into getting me up that mountain.

Sometimes, in the good fight with Jesus, I feel like I'm trailing behind, like I need more water than everyone else, and like I can't get myself up a mountain like I should be able to. My strength goes out. But Jesus is relentless. He refuses to let me turn around when I realize the trail will be impossible, and He refuses to let me not make it up the mountain. Pushing His weight into my back, He whispers, "You and me—we're going to get up this mountain. And we're going to have a deeper understanding of each other than anyone else will ever know because of it."

> *"The LORD is my rock and my fortress and*
> *my deliverer, my God, my rock, in whom I*
> *take refuge, my shield, and the horn of my*
> *salvation, my stronghold."*
> *Psalm 18:2*

I lift up my eyes to the hills.
From where does my help come?
My help comes from the Lord,
who made heaven and earth.
He will not let your foot be moved;
he who keeps you will not slumber.
Behold, he who keeps Israel
will neither slumber nor sleep.
Psalm 121:1-4

bad days welcome here

Some days are just not on our side. Days we are sick. Days we snap at our loved ones without meaning to. Days we cannot possibly get enough sleep. Days too many things go wrong before 8 o'clock in the morning. Days every mess is our own fault, from coffee to communication. Days we don't make it to the social gatherings. Days we can't pull ourselves together. Days that we'll decide can't be fixed.

In my life, I have found that there are two kinds of being humbled—the kind where I stand in awe of God in His place and the kind where I am reminded of mine. The latter is usually more bitter than sweet, but both do the trick.

Bad days are good for the soul. Like a reset of sorts, they put us in our place. They help us remember what it is to be human, to need to sit down sometimes and not take ourselves too seriously. They are the reminder that we don't hold the world together, so we can take a minute when it's needed.

This is a long, long journey with a thousand bad days and growing pains of the heart. And thankfully, Jesus is a God who gets it. I'm pretty sure that if He had a front door and a sign hanging on it, it would read: "Bad days are welcome here." And we need those days, too. Let us remember, we need those days, too.

> *Come to me, all who labor and are heavy*
> *laden, and I will give you rest.*
> *Matthew 11:28*

> *Cast your burden on the LORD, and he will*
> *sustain you; he will never permit*
> *the righteous to be moved.*
> *Psalm 55:22*

untangling

We are so afraid of hard things. We're afraid of complications and chaos and conflict. We're afraid of awkward and uncomfortable. We're afraid of hurting feelings and afraid of being hurt. And even if we think we aren't, we all have limits to our bravery.

But good stories—the victorious kind—take grace and grit and elbow grease. That's the good stuff. The hanging in there, the break through, the figuring it out, the aha!, the dots connecting—but not gracefully or linearly—but like an untangling of necklaces, finally breaking free. Communicating through misunderstanding until we can wear each other's shoes without getting blisters. Wrestling with another complicated, chaotic, intricate, living, breathing, miraculous mystery of a person, and refusing to throw in the towel when it makes no sense to us.

Jesus is a wrestling, through-and-through, to-the-ends-of-the-earth kind of God. I imagine He longs for us to know that we don't have to be afraid of the untangling. We don't have to be afraid of conflict or chaos. After all, what would love be without them? What would relationship be without forgiveness and persistence? What would good be without bad and hard and downright painful?

Keep untangling, dear one. Sometimes it will feel like you're barely going to make it, like it's just near impossible, but that untangling—that hanging in there until the necklaces finally break free—it's the best part.

And let us not grow weary of doing good,
for in due season we will reap, if
we do not give up.
Galatians 6:9

organizing a created thing

It dawned on me in the middle of making a mosaic of broken china dishes that creating has a lot to do with organizing. Whenever I'm laying out a quilt design, I always feel like I'm making a seating chart—choosing which fabrics can sit next to each other and which parts of the family should probably stay on separate sides of the room, if you know what I mean. Creating has a lot do with putting things in their place—putting colors and patterns and textures among their complements, organizing ideas into strains of words, arranging lyrics with notes on the music scale, positioning proportions of facial features in a portrait. The creator of a work is constantly making decisions about placement. Creators are organizers in their beauty making.

Another thing I know to be true about both creating and organizing is that they make a mess. When you clean a room, it generally gets messier in the process. You have to take things out to sort them, clear the nooks and crannies, and put things back in place. Likewise, with creating, you need room to work, and that room is generally a chaotic space—but the best kind of chaotic.

I am not very good at letting people into my chaotic spaces. I like my pieces to be organized before I present them to people. I want them to be as beautiful as I can make them before I let people take them in. In whatever song or piece of art or words I'm making, I don't share projects until they're finished. With creating, it's like a surprise I get to gift my friends and family with, but I realized I also do this with me—my thoughts, feelings, dreams, and the things that make me myself. I try to organize my mess before I share my heart.

But I am a created thing.

Created things can't put themselves into place, because that is the work of the Creator. Jesus is the only One who puts me in my place, and unlike me, He lets people into the chaotic spaces of the creative process. Unlike me, He likes to share me before He's finished. He likes to share my heart as He's making it what it is. It doesn't have to be presentable yet to show the work of the Artist's hand. He glories in my chaos, in my still-being-put-into-place, in my ever-continuing process, because His creations, even in their unfinished states, declare that He is working on something good.

And if my heart and my story are the work of His hands, then who am I to withhold it from others? Who am I to dictate when and how or with whom His art is shared? When I can't for the life of me organize myself and all I want to do is hide until I make myself presentable, He's holding me up in front of others, saying, "Behold! Look at this thing I am making. Can you see that she is going to be good?" But He is not a stranger to that vulnerable feeling in my messy heart. He, too, has been laid bare. So He, Creator, takes care of my heart as I share it because He takes care of the things that are His. And He puts His created things into place without having to prove Himself with a finished work, an organized piece, or a clean room. He can let the world in on His creative chaos and let it be known that though His created things aren't completed yet, they are going to be good.

> *And I am sure of this, that he who began a*
> *good work in you will bring it to*
> *completion at the day of Jesus Christ.*
> *Philippians 1:6*

moon borrowers

"Jesus didn't put you somewhere and forget about you. He didn't lose you. He knows exactly where you are." These were words from a kind stranger combined with words from a sweet friend.

This is why we need people and friendships. They are gold, and they have gold to share. They pick up swords and take up our fight. And they blow us away with their little nuggets of truth and goodness when we've forgotten about our own. My hope is that we never forget about our own treasures and the gold we hold in our hearts. But of course, there will inevitably be times when we need to borrow some goodness, some truth, some hope, some encouragement. I think that's the point—that we share when we have, borrow when we need, and lend back whenever possible. I think Jesus was a friend of borrowers just as much as He was a friend of investors. He's a fan of laying down troubles and not doing things alone. He's a fan of sharing the weight of both burden and blessing. He's just not a stingy kind of God. So He made us each other.

And like borrowing the moon for the night while the other side of the world borrows the sun for a day, or a little kid asking for the blue crayon and offering the yellow one in its stead, we are borrowers of grace and goodness, bold prayers and kind words, reformation and a tiny bit of courage. When we share and when we borrow, we'll remember that Jesus didn't lose us. He knows exactly where we are—smack dab in the middle of living, breathing, speaking reminders of Himself.

Two are better than one, because they have
a good reward for their toil. For if they fall,
one will lift up his fellow. But woe to him
who is alone when he falls and has not
another to lift him up!
Ecclesiastes 4:9-10

For I do not mean that others should be
eased and you burdened, but that as a
matter of fairness your abundance at the
present time should supply their need, so
that their abundance may supply your
need, that there may be fairness.
2 Corinthians 8:13-14

And let us consider how to stir up one
another to love and good works, not
neglecting to meet together, as is the habit
of some, but encouraging one another...
Hebrews 10:24-25

going small

The Lord is a mind-blower. He's unconventional and out of the box. But I am convinced that He goes small. I know creating a universe is not a small feat, but I think Jesus went small with you and me and a fruit tree. And I think He went small with a manger birth and a criminal's death. He had a home team of twelve, and He kept Himself a secret from as many people as He could, begging the healed not to tell anyone whom they'd met. He snuck away to pray in gardens. And He had best friends, closer-than-mosts.

I think it's easy for us to think of Jesus with five thousand people surrounding Him at all times, and it paints an image of this God who goes so, so big and then goes home. But Jesus said where two or three are gathered, there He is among them. Literally just two. You and me, and He's there. And here's the thing—this Church, the Bride—is mega, but She goes small. She gathers in twos and threes and twelves. I think the Bride is one who calls people by name and by heart. I think She is life-on-life and face-to-face because that's who Jesus was. I don't think She lets people stay strangers or acquaintances for long. She knows deeply, wrestles persistently, and goes small.

So, grab another half of two, speak face-to-face and heart-to-heart, and find Jesus in your midst. After all, He is a human-dweller anyway. Find Him in each other. Because, Church, that's the good stuff.

> *Again I say to you, if two of you agree on earth about anything they ask, it will be done for them by my Father in heaven. For where two or three are gathered in my name, there am I among them.*
> *Matthew 18:19-20*

tender-hearted

I remember the first time I ever cried happy tears. I was listening to a beautiful friend talk about beautiful things and love and people, and I was so inspired and so filled with joy that it just leaked. Those are the best tears— the ones that sneak up on you because you're witnessing something so beautiful that it makes you cry. As if the body can't contain the beauty the heart is taking in, it just leaks out.

As far as I know, Scripture only refers to Jesus weeping in sorrow, and while it says there will be no crying in Heaven, I cannot imagine a Jesus or a Heaven without happy tears. Far be it from me to rewrite Scripture, and I could be dead wrong, but I think My God, who is more full of mirth than we could handle, knows what it's like to cry over beautiful things—to just leak out. I think Jesus knows all the tears—the good ones and the sweet ones, the rich ones and the funny ones, the devastating ones and the fearful ones. And I think Jesus loves us face-to-face, the way leaking hearts do, with tenderness.

Tender is one of my all time favorite words because tender hearts are the ones that give and love and live, and have also known loss and pain and injustice. They've been stretched and pushed and exercised without becoming so strong that they don't feel the activity, like quad muscles on day ten of half-marathon training. They are exposed, but not calloused, like out-of-practice fingers on guitar strings. There's a sweet spot between not enough and too much, like chicken that's cooked but not overdone or pasta al dente. I think Jesus is in that sweet spot.

One of the things that has always amazed me about Jesus is that He knew He was going to raise Lazarus from the dead moments later, and He still took a moment to weep and mourn with Mary. That's the Jesus I know—a tender One. Oh, I think He is strong and steady, but I think His heart is always on the edge, always on the brink of tears, teetering right between joy and sadness, so that no matter what the occasion calls for, He's there in a moment's notice, fully present, wholly sufficient.

Oh, how I want to love like that—face-to-face, leaking heart, and always full and ready for every kind of occasion.

Jesus said to her, "Your brother will rise again." When Jesus saw her weeping, and the Jews who had come with her also weeping, he was deeply moved in his spirit and greatly troubled. And he said, "Where have you laid him?" They said to him, "Lord, come and see." Jesus wept.
John 11:23, v. 33-35

Love is...
(a musician's 1 Corinthians 13)

I can be one of the greats, but without Love—the Musician of musicians, I am nothing but dissonant.

I can play all the right notes, but without Love, I will never make a sound.

Love doesn't rush the tempo; it is the beautiful pace.

Love tunes itself to others; it is pleasing to the ear.

Love is not in the melody line—it is the harmonies that come together to make each other beautiful in a richer, more powerful sound.

Love is the crescendo, the glory of glories, the power of a thousand voices;

And it is the silence at the end that strikes you strange, unresolved and gentle as a whisper.

we the harmonizers

You know those friends who teach you something immeasurable about one thing they do like none other—one specialty of theirs? I have a friend who knows the fierce and unmatched power of God unlike anyone else I have met. The first time we played worship together, I jumped in with the harmony, and she said it was as if horses were bursting out of gates at the start of a race. Harmonies have become my favorite thing to sing because while there is such sweetness in them, there is also power.

It is nearly impossible to harmonize without hearing the other person—even as you sing your own notes, you have to continually listen to your counterpart. And the notes, in their own positions on the scales, are not the same, but they make each other stronger. They move together, making a more powerful sound together than apart. It is pleasing to the ear.

I think Jesus is a harmonizer. I don't think He takes the melody. I think He listens constantly to us. And even though He doesn't change, I think He moves Himself on the scale to meet us in our melodies. He left Heaven to walk this

Earth with human skin and breathe the oxygen we breathe just to be with us—in sync, side-by-side, in our melody. And when He jumps in with that harmony, the power is unmatched, like horses bursting out of gates at the start of a race.

Oh, sweet ones, whenever possible, let us be harmonizers. Let us meet others in their melodies. Let us listen closely and constantly to our counterparts and join them in the song they're singing. And together, may we make a sound more beautiful than we can fathom.

But whoever would be great among you
must be your servant, and whoever would
be first among you must be your slave, even
as the Son of Man came not to be served
but to serve, and to give his life
as a ransom for many.
Matthew 20:26-28

i get you

We sat there talking about our seasons, three of us from three different places in life: One of us had just gotten married, one of us had just moved back home from college, and one of us was in nursing school. Something happens to friendships when someone celebrates a milestone or enters a new season—there is an unspoken misassumption that we've now become unable to relate to each other. I remember feeling ridiculously vulnerable as I talked about what it was like to feel lonely and unqualified and just small, and I remember being astonished as they, too, in their own words shared similar feelings.

In that season after college, I found myself "losing it" often, forgoing my composure, and just telling the truth about things. And I found that I was more understood than I ever thought or imagined. No one ever heard my thoughts and said, "I've never felt that way before." Instead, I was met by "I get you," and "Me too." I'm convinced that those are some of the most powerful words in the world. That's why God became flesh and walked around on Earth, isn't it? So that He could say, "I get you," and, "Me too." The Lord made us human in every season, and He made us with the ability to relate to each other. He made us to share, to understand, and to "I get you," so that we know that no one is alone. And since we're not alone, we don't have to have to do our seasons by ourselves. We don't have to do anything by ourselves—that's the beauty of a God who says, "I get you" and created a multitude of His image-bearers who can say, "I get you," too.

Again, if two lie together, they keep
warm, but how can one keep warm
alone? And though a man might prevail
against one who is alone, two will
withstand him—a threefold cord
is not quickly broken.
Ecclesiastes 4:11-12

No temptation has overtaken you that is
not common to man.
1 Corinthians 10:13

For we do not have a high priest who is
unable to sympathize with our weaknesses,
but one who in every respect has
been tempted as we are, yet without sin.
Hebrews 4:15

the time we missed church & remembered

We literally couldn't find parking. There was a marching band competition at the high school where our church held its services, and the streets were full for more blocks than we could count. Given that we were going on thirty minutes late, I thought of an alternative and said, "I have an idea. Let's go home." So the three of us sat outside on the balcony of my apartment with our Bibles and chocolate and talked about how we were. How we *really* were. We confessed the things that were filling our hearts with what's worthless instead of what's precious. For me, that week, it was Netflix. It isn't always, but that day, it really, really was. I said, "As silly as it sounds, I have to stop watching Netflix for a little while. I need more time in the Word, and I need more time talking to Jesus. Will you help me?"

We talked about being watchful and thankful and about how the littlest, most unworthy things can disrupt that sometimes. And we vowed to fight together for the precious things—to remember the things that we know deep down are better than gold. We reminded each other where we've been, and we connected each other's dots. My sweet friend always says I connect her dots for her. I think that's why Jesus made friendship, and I think it's why He made the Church. We're better together. We're more watchful and more thankful, and we remember more.

I have no idea what the sermon we missed was about that day, but I will always remember deeply and gratefully the time a marching band competition kept us from church and made us remember.

Devote yourselves to prayer, being
watchful and thankful.
Colossians 4:2

For you are all children of light, children of
the day. We are not of the night or of the
darkness. So then let us not sleep, as others
do, but let us keep awake and be sober.
Therefore encourage one another and build
one another up, just as you are doing.
1 Thessalonians 5:5-6, v.11

potlucks & the kingdom of God

We were sitting next to each other on the bus to Athens in Greece, talking about what we think the kingdom of Heaven is like. My friend said he always thought of Heaven like a potluck—like people gathering around in backyard circles, communing over a meal made up of everyone's mutually necessary contributions.

I loved that, even though I had never really been a fan of potlucks. I always feel nervous cooking for other people. I love deviating from recipes, combining my own ingredients, and forgoing measuring cups, and I am always afraid that other people won't like what I make. Taste preferences are different, and nothing is ever everybody's cup of tea. But the thing about potlucks is that we do them together—each and every one of us.

I think every person brings something to this table, a piece of value and of relationship to this gathering. No two relationships with the Lord are alike. We all see and know different parts of God's heart differently. I have a friend who knows God's gentleness like no one else I've ever met. I have another friend who knows God's compassion; another who knows His protection; another who knows His ever-constant invitation like I've never known; and the list is endless. The beauty of that is that we can never run out of things to know about God. We never run out of facets of His character or nooks and crannies of His heart.

And when I think of potlucks and the Kingdom of God, I think of bringing our resources to one table, piecing together the bits that we know about, and sharing our little portion so that we all may see the bigger picture. I don't know much about collard greens or haggis, and there are certainly more things for me to learn about God, but I make a mean almond cupcake and a dozen variations of pasta, so please, please, let us each bring our dishes to the potluck, our stories to the gathering, and our plates to the table.

For just as the body is one and has many
members, and all the members of the body,
though many, are one body,
so it is with Christ.
1 Corinthians 12:12

airport reunions

There are few things in this life I find more precious than airport reunions. I am convinced that three of the most powerful sentiments we could ever say to someone are found in that arrival section of the airport that people walk through before they reach the baggage claim.

"Welcome."

"I've missed you."

"I'm here."

Every time I see a person looking for his or her traveler, whether they've met once or been married forty years, it reminds me of Jesus. I can just see Jesus standing at the bottom of the escalator, extending His neck to look around the crowd, as pure relief and delight sweep over His face the second He lays eyes on us. And He probably brought flowers or maybe a coffee thermos, and He gives us a really firm, longer-than-usual embrace, saying, "Welcome back. I'm so glad you made it safely. I hope you had a great time. But also, life wasn't the same without you. Please don't ever be away that long again." Then we walk to the baggage claim, us with the coffee and He ready to grab the suitcases, and He goes on to catch us up on things we missed—"It rained three inches; I picked up fresh groceries; I kept the house clean while you were gone," all just another way of saying, "I'm so glad you're here."

I've seen quite a few wonders on this planet, and I've dipped my toes into some oceans from even more continents, but in all of the world, the most beautiful of sights I've seen is people getting excited about people. I think Jesus dwells in those moments. It's His heart—to be excited about people and to watch us be excited about them, too.

Beloved, let us love one another, for love is
from God, and whoever loves has been born
of God and knows God... No one has ever
seen God; if we love one another, God
abides in us and his love is perfected in us.
1 John 4:7, v. 12

mirrors by nature

A beautifully fierce Haitian woman I got to do life alongside for a few weeks said that you can never call anybody ugly because that's like saying God is ugly. Oh, how I wish we knew that the image of God can never be ugly and that we cannot call ugly something that He has called beautiful.

It was ingrained in me that humanity is depraved, wretched, sinful by nature. By nature—as in, we can't help it. We are not good by nature, but sinful, and in need of the grace of God. Oh, undoubtedly I believe that we need the grace of God, and I believe that we cannot be good without Goodness Himself. But we are also image-bearers—mirrors, so to speak. Even when a mirror breaks, its nature is not brokenness. It is still a mirror by nature. We may be the broken image of God, but we were still designed, by nature, to be the image of God. The truth of who we are—by God's good, good design—is beautiful, image-bearing, capable, adept, filled with life and power. No amount of broken can take the image of God out of us.

Let us remember that the death we experience in our broken state is the work of a liar, but the life in our bones was breathed by a truth-speaker, and He called it good. The heart of the truth-speaking God I know bends and breaks for His good, good creation.

Jesus only makes beautiful people. Every single one. There is no other kind of person. I think when God gave His Son, He gave His heart, that we might have His heart. Though there are a lot of things I don't know about Jesus' heart, here's one that I do—He likes people. I mean, like really, really likes them. I'm not talking about He secretly finds them annoying, but puts kindness first because it's the right thing to do. I don't think Jesus does anything He doesn't want to. And let's be real, you don't go through hell for someone unless you like them. Even the people we struggle to like—He's crazy about them. His heart is bursting out of the seams of Heaven for them. And when He gave His heart, He meant for it to burst in us, too. And this bursting heart breaks when His creation speaks lies over each other or about each other—lies like stupidity or incompetence or anything less than beautiful.

I wasn't there, but I don't think Jesus called His disciples fools the way we do. I don't think He was calling them idiots. I think His heart broke when He said it. I think it was crying out, "You don't know what you're missing, and how I wish you did. You don't know the life I created you for and the life I want to keep creating in you, my good, good design." His good, good design, which no matter how broken, is still, in nature, a mirror, made in the likeness of God Himself.

*...whoever insults his brother will be liable
to the council; and whoever says, 'You fool!'
will be liable to the hell of fire.*
Matthew 5:22

*...but no human being can tame the tongue.
It is a restless evil, full of deadly
poison. With it we bless our Lord and
Father, and with it we curse people who are
made in the likeness of God.*
James 3:8-9

the miracles under our feet

We were staying in the apartment above the church in Piraeus, Greece while a wedding was going on in the sanctuary downstairs. We were looking out our windows excitedly trying to see whatever we could of a Greek wedding, when one of my teammates said there was a miracle taking place under our feet. "Two people deciding to love each other for a lifetime—I think that's a miracle," she said.

I think so, too. I think every time we decide to love someone is a miracle. It's a miracle when we bite our tongues whenever hurtful words flash through our minds, when we say the things that are hard to say because they're important, when we step into another person's shoes or thoughts in hopes that we can understand the world like that person does, when we cancel our plans for solo time because someone needs or deserves a listening ear, when we decide to do something a different way because it's how another person likes to do it. Every time we clean up a mess we didn't make, cook a meal for someone else, or see a person's heart and find beauty—I think that's a miracle.

After everything that has happened since the beginning of time to tear us apart and turn us against one another, the fact that we can love at all, even thirty seconds at a time, is a miracle. The fact that we can see even glimpses of the preciousness and the sacredness of another human being, after evil has clouded our view like smog in the city of stars, is a miracle—a work of God. Love and people and loving people are God's work, and us bearing witness to that is purely miraculous.

Beloved, let us love one another, for love is from God, and whoever loves has been born of God and knows God. Anyone who does not love does not know God, because God is love.
1 John 4:7-8

the remnant

Every artist, no matter how appreciated, knows what it's like to also be unappreciated. The same is true for writers and speakers and every human brave enough to share something of him or herself. The good, precious, most profound, utterly necessary truths go missed sometimes—a lot of times, actually. How many times do people just flat out miss Jesus and His gospel and the truth and the goodness that He is? They see it and hear it, but just miss it. Like in Scripture when He says you have ears but can't hear and eyes but can't see.[2] The good things and the precious things just get missed. How many times did I miss them before Jesus put them in my heart? Jesus is the most undervalued, unappreciated, rejected artist of all time. People walk right past Him and don't realize what they're missing, or they see His work and devalue it or attribute it to other things.

---

[2] Mark 8:18

Something dawned on me as I was thinking about the Creator of the world being the most rejected and misunderstood artist of all time. Thirty-one percent[3] of the world today is comprised of people who profess to be "Christians," which includes the Roman Catholic, Orthodox, Anglican and Non-denominational religions. It includes the people who say they believe in Jesus but have never talked to Him, the ones who go to church on Sundays but never open His word on their own, and the ones who do talk to Him and read His word, but don't let it have any effect on the way they live or love. So regardless of the actual number, the percentage of the people who know and love Jesus is small. And that's at our current point in time, when there are the most Christians there have ever been in the world and the most biblical translations there have ever been.

I thought about how many billions of people have lived in the last few millenniums and how many of those probably actually knew Jesus, not the ones that Jesus says He'll see and say, "I never knew you."[4] And something hit me like I'd never known before.

At the end of this whole thing, Jesus doesn't get back most of His creation. Most of the people He created, He doesn't actually get back; He just keeps a remnant. And

---

[3] Hackett, Conrad, and David McClendon. "Christians Remain World's Largest Religious Group, but They Are Declining in Europe." Pew Research Center, 5 Apr. 2017, www.pewresearch.org/fact-tank/2017/04/05/christians-remain-worlds-largest-religious-group-but-they-are-declining-in-europe/.

[4] Matthew 7:21-23

He still wins. It's still His victory. Even though He loses most of His people, He still wins because He is still He and good is still good.

I thought about Noah and how God regretted that He made man, and He wanted to destroy them all, but Noah was the one person who found favor with Him, so He did it all over again—the whole thing—which affected millenniums of people afterward. Because of one person. And then He died for them. He literally went through hell for the remnant of people that wouldn't. He did the whole thing for His remnant. Because that's the kind of Creator He is. The kind who never gets back the majority of His creation, whom He loves to death, but who considers His remnant a victory, an inheritance, His portion and His lot. And for the remnant, He's like, "Man, are you in for the best thing ever." He just—gives everything—and the whole time He knew He'd get a remnant. He wanted all of them, of course, but He knew how many more people would spend eternity without Him than with Him. And He did the whole thing anyway.

So, you and me, if you know and love this Jesus—we are the remnant of the Treasure of the world. We hold the Treasure of the world in our souls—the most we could ever gain from this life, the ultimate prize and reward, is in our hearts. We have Him, and He has us, His remnant, His reward. So what's left for someone who already holds the Treasure of the world in his or her soul? Show the world its Treasure. Give everything you can to let others have this Treasure. Lord knows that's what He did.

*The LORD saw that the wickedness of
man was great in the earth, and that
every intention of the thoughts of his heart
was only evil continually. And the LORD
regretted that he had made man on the
earth, and it grieved him to his heart. So
the LORD said, "I will blot out man whom I
have created from the face of the land, man
and animals and creeping things and birds
of the heavens, for I am sorry that I have
made them." But Noah found favor in the
eyes of the LORD.*
Genesis 6:5-8

*...the mystery hidden for ages and
generations but now revealed to his
saints. To them God chose to make known
how great among the Gentiles are the
riches of the glory of this mystery, which is
Christ in you, the hope of glory. Him we
proclaim, warning everyone and teaching
everyone with all wisdom, that we may
present everyone mature in Christ.*
Colossians 1:26-28

*So too at the present time there is a
remnant, chosen by grace.*
Romans 11:5

To my Treasure and Sweetest Friend,
all of my pages are Yours.
You blew me away again.
"Thank you" doesn't even begin to cover it,
but with every breath,
thank You for making Your home with me.

Made in the USA
Lexington, KY
08 June 2018